*Join the thousands of people
who have transformed their lives
in less than a month!*

**NEW &
REVISED**

21 DAY

INNER
HEALING

JOURNEY

A PERSONAL GUIDE TO HEALING PAST HURTS
AND BECOMING EMOTIONALLY HEALTHY

BESTSELLING AUTHOR

JIMMY EVANS

DEDICATION

To my granddaughters Abby, Elle, and Kate.

21 Day Inner Healing Journey:
A Personal Guide to Healing Past Hurts
and Becoming Emotionally Healthy

Copyright © 2021 XO Publishing.
All rights reserved.

P.O Box 59888
Dallas, Texas 75229
1-800-380-6330
Or visit our website at xomarriage.com

XO Publishing

ISBN: 978-1-950113-61-3 Paperback
ISBN: 978-1-950113-62-0 eBook
ISBN: 978-1-950113-67-5 Audiobook

Printed in the United States of America

CONTENTS

INTRODUCTION

Welcome to your journey to healing. I'm glad you have joined me. *The purpose of this journey is for you to allow the Lord to heal you in every area of your life.* You already know your personal broken and hurting places, and you're running those through your mind as you begin reading here. Some wounds you carry from your childhood, while others happened to you once you got older. You have been through some difficult times, and you weren't always sure how to respond. That is true for all of us. Words were spoken. Actions were taken. People entered or left your life. You may have caused others pain through sin or mistakes. In any case, you are here right now, nursing emotional and spiritual scars, and sometimes even open wounds.

You are aware of your condition, and you know you should be in a better place than you are right now because those wounds and scars prevent you from being the person God wants you to be.

I became a Christian over 48 years ago, and the Lord healed me, but I didn't start out that way. In my growing years, my parents had not yet become Christians, so I was unaware of the good things God could do in my life. On top of that, I acted out with terrible rebellion and immorality. I finally turned to Christ and became a believer at nineteen, but all my problems didn't end there. I was still carrying deep wounds. It took a lot of years for the Lord to heal me, but it shouldn't have taken that long. The only reason I stayed in pain like I did was because no one gave me the type of resource you are reading right now. In fact, when Jesus saved me, I didn't even know I *could* find the kind of healing you will learn about in this book. I needlessly struggled with my pain for many years, and it needlessly delayed me from becoming the person God wanted me to be.

When I married my wife, Karen, almost 50 years ago, I was devastated by the way I grew up, and it had a terrible impact on my wife. Yes, we loved each other, but the pain I carried took a toll on our marriage. When the Lord began to heal our hearts, it took us several years to experience complete healing.

Although I needlessly lived unhealed for many years, you don't have to have the same experience. I finally learned about the healing Jesus made available to me, and it changed my life. It's going to change yours also.

In this journey, you will take a deep look at many areas of your life as I share what I learned from my own journey to healing. Over the next twenty-one days, you will begin to see God in a new way that will transform your life and every relationship in it. This is a big deal!

First, I encourage you *not to go too quickly* because the journey may take longer than you expect. Let God take over and do what He wants to do in your heart. You may need to take several days on a particular lesson, and it may take you even more time to process some things. Work at your own pace but allow God enough time to work. I also urge you to go back through the process when you want and need to do it. You can do it more than once or just go through select lessons again. Let God keep doing a deep work in your life. Second, *don't skip days* because they all build on each other, though I will repeat some important concepts when they apply. Finally, *work through the exercises* throughout each day. These exercises are particularly important to help you apply what you learn.

We will spend a lot of time together on this journey, but in the end, I believe you will find complete healing. You will change, and a different person will emerge—the person God made you to be.

Father, I thank You for my friends who are joining me on this journey. I pray You will bless them and be with them on the way. I ask You to heal them completely so they can love, follow, and live for You. Lead each one to become the person you created them to be. In Jesus' name, amen.

A VERY IMPORTANT QUESTION

Before we begin this journey together, I have an especially important personal question to ask you. In fact, it is the most important question anyone will ever ask you.

Have you invited Jesus into your heart to be your Lord and Savior?

If your answer is "yes" to that question, then you can skip to Day One.

If your answer is "no," then I need to tell you that it is particularly important for you to invite Jesus into your heart at this time. This journey will not help you, at least not in the best way, unless you surrender to Jesus and have a personal relationship with Him.

Here are some important Scriptures to help you understand as you take this critical step:

For by grace you have been saved through faith, and that not of yourselves; it is the gift of God, not of works, lest anyone should boast. (Ephesians 2:8–9)

Behold, I stand at the door and knock. If anyone hears My voice and opens the door, I will come in to him and dine with him, and he with Me. (Revelation 3:20)

For God so loved the world that He gave His only begotten Son, that whoever believes in Him should not perish but have everlasting life. For God did not send His Son into the world to condemn the world, but that the world through Him might be saved. He who believes in Him is not condemned; but he who does not believe is condemned already, because he has not believed in the name of the only begotten Son of God. (John 3:16–18)

Salvation (being saved) is an act of grace we don't deserve. God offers it as a gift that we receive instantly when we open our hearts to Jesus and allow Him into our lives to save us from our sins and be our Lord. God loves you personally and wants to have a personal relationship with you. When you open your heart to Jesus and invite Him in, He will forgive you for all your sins, give you the gift of eternal life in Heaven forever, live in your heart, and personally relate to you. He does all this because of His great love for you. This love is not something God has for us because we deserve it. He loves us because He created us in our mothers' wombs (see Psalm 139), and we are His children, made in His image.

Jesus died for us on the cross to pay for our sins and break the power of sin over our lives. He did this because sin was keeping us away from God, and there was no way we could deal with our sin problem on our own. Knowing that we were helpless in our sins, God sent Jesus, His only Son, to die in our place and pay for our sins so He could remove them forever.

When we receive Jesus into our lives, we lay claim to the forgiveness, freedom, and blessings Jesus died and rose again from the dead to give us. All these blessings flow from our personal relationship with Him. If you are ready to receive Jesus into your heart at this time, then say this prayer to Him:

Jesus, I confess that I have sinned against You, and I repent. I open my heart to You and ask You to come into my life to be my Lord and Savior. I submit my life to You, and from this day forward, I will live to serve You. I believe You have come into my heart and have forgiven my sins. I believe and trust You have now saved me by your grace and given me the gift of eternal life. Jesus, I pray You will fill me with Your Holy Spirit and give me the power to change, to know You, and to live my life for You. Amen!

If you said that prayer, then you know now that Jesus is in your heart as the Lord of your life. This prayer is the most important of your life and changes your eternity. It is also common after you pray this prayer for the devil to try to tell you it isn't real or you are too bad to be forgiven. Don't worry, that happens to almost everyone. In this journey, you will learn how to distinguish the devil's voice from God's voice and how to overcome the devil. You can be certain that you are now a child of God, a Christian, and a fellow member of God's family. Welcome!

It is important for a new believer to submit to water baptism as an act of obedience to Jesus. It is the first thing Jesus commands us to do as new believers as a token of our sincerity and obedience to Him (see Mark 16:15–16; Matthew 28:19–20). If you don't have a home church, then find a Bible-believing church and tell someone there that you would like to be water baptized. Be committed to a church, attend regularly, and get involved. It is important to your new faith to be around fellow believers who can encourage you in the things of God.

SECTION ONE

THE RIGHT CONCEPT OF GOD

For this journey, we must begin at the beginning—and I mean the very beginning. Before anything else was created, there was God. When humans rebelled against God and began to sin, it only makes sense that the first thing that was affected was their understanding of God.

Here you are, at the beginning of this journey, and if you are going to start on the right foot, then the place to begin is with your concept of God. Your healing is going to occur as the Lord touches your heart. And for that to happen you have to trust Him enough to allow Him to have access to the most sensitive and sacred areas of your soul. If your concept of God has been distorted or damaged it will cause you to believe things about God that aren't true and even to doubt His love. Therefore, we begin at this critical place in the journey to inner healing.

Day 1

A Good God

Our problem usually begins here: We have a wrong concept of God. In the Bible's first book, God created the earth and everything in it, including humans. That is the first and best part of the story, but then it goes downhill from there. The devil (in the form of a serpent) came into the beautiful garden God had created and approached the first two human beings, Adam and Eve. The first thing the serpent hissed out of his mouth were two devilish lies: God is not good, and God is not loving. Once they swallowed those poisonous concepts and believed them, they sinned. Then, they hid in shame because they evidently did not believe that God would forgive them. Here is the way Genesis describes this terrible event:

> *Now the serpent was more cunning than any beast of the field which the Lord God had made. And he said to the woman, "Has God indeed said, 'You shall not eat of every tree of the garden'?"*
>
> *And the woman said to the serpent, "We may eat the fruit of the trees of the garden; but of the fruit of the tree which is in the midst of the garden, God has said,*

'You shall not eat it, nor shall you touch it, lest you die.'"

Then the serpent said to the woman, "You will not surely die. For God knows that in the day you eat of it your eyes will be opened, and you will be like God, knowing good and evil." (Genesis 3:1–5)

You can see that the first action the devil took was to accuse God, and Adam and Eve believed him. Based on the devil's deception, they ate the fruit from the forbidden tree. After that, God came looking for them, but they had gone into hiding (Genesis 3:6–9).

In their attempt to escape God's eyes, the two humans gathered fig leaves to cover their nakedness—and their shame.

Then the Lord God called to Adam and said to him, "Where are you?"

So he said, "I heard Your voice in the garden, and I was afraid because I was naked; and I hid myself."

And He said, "Who told you that you were naked? Have you eaten from the tree of which I commanded you that you should not eat?"

Then the man said, "The woman whom You gave to be with me, she gave me of the tree, and I ate."

And the Lord God said to the woman, "What is this you have done?"
The woman said, "The serpent deceived me, and I ate." (Genesis 3:9–13)

Do you see what the devil did here? He came to Eve and told her that God was both a bully and a liar. The serpent edited the story and said that even if God did tell her that if she ate of the fruit of the tree she would die, the truth was that she and Adam would be better off. They would be like God.

Here in this first lesson, I want you to understand that you can only get as close to God as your concept of Him will allow. If you begin your journey thinking God is neither good nor loving, then this will be a long and bumpy ride. Why? Because you might think you're letting Him get close enough to you to hurt you, but what you're really doing is *preventing* Him from helping you.

God is your Healer, but if you hide like Adam and Eve, then you are hiding from the only one who can truly help you.

I am here to tell you that *God is a good God.* He is nothing like the devil said. Even so, like Adam and Eve, many times we find it easier to believe a lie than to accept the truth. Most of us develop our first concepts of God from our parents as we grow up. God stamped His image on Adam and Eve, and then He commanded them to multiply (or procreate). Parents, then, are the image-bearers of God. He entrusted them with the responsibility of leading their children into an understanding of God and a relationship with Him. When it happens, it's beautiful. However, many of us didn't grow up in homes that did that. Even if we had good parents, they weren't perfect. The issue is that we naturally attribute the actions of our parents to God. If, for example, we had generous, loving, kind, and moral parents, then we tend to think of God in those ways. On the other hand, we also naturally attribute the things they do wrong to God. If we had distant, uncaring, legalistic, and abusive parents, then we are apt to think of God in those terms.

Our parents, for good or bad, become the filter by which we view God.

The problem is that seeing God through the lens of our parents' actions distorts our view, and we do not see Him as He really is. As I was growing up, I had good parents, but they were very distant in many ways. My father did not attend any of my sporting events. He was never involved in my day-to-day life. As a result, when I became an adult, I struggled with all these wounds that needed healing. It was incredibly difficult for me to believe that God could really love me.

The purpose of this lesson is to repair the faulty concept that God is not good. If you have been holding on to that idea, ask yourself these two questions: *What did my parents do right?*

5

And what did they do wrong? Which of those actions or characteristics have you attributed to God? I present these questions because you need to be able to disassociate your parents' behavior from who God is and what He does. I especially want you to be able to read the things Jesus says about God the Father in the Gospels without the filter of your earthly parents.

Regardless of what your parents thought or think about you, God is crazy in love with you. He loves you more than you can comprehend. The Bible says God's perfect love casts out our fears (1 John 4:18). In fact, His perfect love will heal your heart. God wants to do a magnificent work in your life because He loves you. As I heard one preacher say, "God loves you just the way you are, but He also loves you too much to let you stay that way." He wants to bring healing into your life because He is so incredibly good.

HEALING FROM GOD'S WORD

Therefore I say to you, do not worry about your life, what you will eat or what you will drink; nor about your body, what you will put on. Is not life more than food and the body more than clothing? Look at the birds of the air, for they neither sow nor reap nor gather into barns; yet your heavenly Father feeds them. Are you not of more value than they? Which of you by worrying can add one cubit to his stature?

So why do you worry about clothing? Consider the lilies of the field, how they grow: they neither toil nor spin; and yet I say to you that even Solomon in all his glory was not arrayed like one of these. Now if God so clothes the grass of the field, which today is, and tomorrow is thrown into the oven, will He *not much more* clothe *you, O you of little faith?*

Therefore do not worry, saying, "What shall we eat?" or "What shall we drink?" or 'What shall we wear?' For after all these things the Gentiles seek. For your heavenly Father knows that you need all these things... (Matthew 6:25-32)

In that day you will ask in My name, and I do not say to you that I shall pray the Father for you; for the Father Himself loves you, because you have loved Me, and have believed that I came forth from God. I came forth from the Father and have come into the world. Again, I leave the world and go to the Father. (John 16:26-28)

Let your conduct be without covetousness; be content with such things as you have. For He Himself has said, "I will never leave you nor forsake you." So we may boldly say: "The Lord is my helper; I will not fear. What can man do to me?" (Hebrews 13:5-6)

HEALING TRUTHS

- Only God can heal you from life's hurts and the attacks of the devil, such as shame and fear. If you try to hide from Him, then you are running from your Healer, which is what the devil wants to happen. The devil wants to deceive you about who God is so he can convince you that He is a liar and a bully. If the devil can succeed in his lies, he can keep you defeated and separated from God.

- You can only get as close to God as your concept of Him will allow. Because the devil lied to Adam and Eve about God and got them to embrace shame after they fell, they hid from God rather than looking for Him. If you believe the devil's lies about God, then you won't go to God for help. Instead, you fear Him and can't believe He loves you. You begin to believe He only sees your faults, and He wants to condemn you.

- You develop your primary concept of God from your parents. In Genesis chapter 1, God placed His image on Adam and Eve and commanded them to multiply. The primary role of parents is to be image-bearers of God to their children. Their first responsibility is to lead their children into a proper understanding of God and to help them build a relationship with Him. Since parents are the first image children have of God, whatever they do—right or wrong—their children will naturally attribute to God.

• If you want God to heal you, then you must first heal your image of Him. This healing begins to take place as you conduct two tasks. First, you must disassociate your concept of God from your parents and any other authority figure, religious or otherwise, who led you to skew your concept of God. Second, read the Bible and believe what it says about God as opposed to filtering your view of Him through past experiences.

• God is a merciful, gracious, and caring Father who adores you despite your problems, hurts, or sins. He will gently love you, forgive you, and heal you if you come to Him by faith.

Exercises for Reflection and Discussion

1. How would you describe your concept of God? Do you believe He loves and accepts you? Why or why not?

_____

_____

_____

_____

_____

_____

2. What do you think your parents did that positively affected your concept of God?

_____

_____

_____

_____

_____

_____

3. What do you think your parents did that negatively affected your concept of God?

_____

_____

_____

_____

_____

_____

4. If parents did things that negatively affected your concept of God, how has this inhibited or changed your ability to relate to God and trust Him?

_____

_____

_____

_____

_____

Applying Healing Principles

Complete the following steps to apply what you have learned in the lesson:

1. **Forgive your parents for their failures. This is essential in beginning your healing journey.**

2. **Differentiate and disassociate your parents' failures from your concept of God and allow Him to be your perfect heavenly Father without limiting Him through the filter of your past experiences.**

3. **Draw close to God in prayer and trust Him as your perfect Father despite your past or your feelings.**

4. **Distinguish and disassociate your concept of God from people in your past who may have negatively influenced your concept of Him, including abusive, legalistic, or ungodly authority or religious figures.**

Healing Confession

Confess the following aloud.

I confess and agree with God's Word that my perfect Heavenly Father loves me. He accepts me because of the sacrifice Jesus made for me by His death on the cross. Therefore, I know God has forgiven my sins, and He completely accepts me and loves me. He cares about every detail of my life, and I can trust Him with all my needs, desires, hurts, problems, and sins. He will never leave me nor forsake me.

Healing Prayer

In Matthew's Gospel, Jesus taught us how to begin our prayers with what is commonly known as the Lord's Prayer. He said, *"In this manner, therefore, pray: Our Father in heaven, Hallowed be Your name"* (Matthew 6:9). The Greek word translated "hallowed" means to cleanse or sanctify. When we begin our prayers this way, we tell God we want Him to cleanse our hearts and minds of anything that keeps us from seeing Him as He truly is. We commit to living our lives in a manner that honors and glorifies Him. I personally say this prayer every day in my quiet time, which I will talk about near the end of this book.

This prayer we offer today is the beginning of our journey to know God intimately as He reveals who He really is to us. Pray this prayer silently or aloud:

Good Father, I want to know You for who You really are. I realize I have held misconceptions about You because of my past. I forgive my parents or anyone else who has confused or deceived me about who You are. My prayer today is that You will hallow Your Name to me. I pray You will cleanse my heart and mind of anything that keeps me from knowing You. Today, I choose to begin the lifelong pursuit of seeking and knowing You. I believe what the Bible says about You, regardless of my hurts from the past or what my emotions might try to tell me. As I take this journey to emotional healing and health, I want to take it with You. I am believing You for total healing in my life. What I need is too much for me or any other person to do, but it isn't too much for You. I believe You love me and accept me. I believe You are with me and will never leave nor forsake me. You are my best friend and perfect Father. I ask You today to heal my heart and my concept of who You are. In Jesus' name, amen.

Day 2

A Loving God

Once we get our hearts and minds straightened out about God's goodness, we need the Holy Spirit to repair our concept of His love. In the English language and in Western culture, we overuse and misuse the word *love*, throwing it around so much that it means everything and nothing. We might love our pajamas. We love our parents. We may love our sports team. We love our spouses. We could love hot dogs. Or we love pizza. We throw the word love around casually, and yet, many of our deepest hurts come from people who told us they loved us but didn't always act in loving ways. We may have even heard that God loves us, but the concept of His love gets mixed and muddled into all the people who have ever said they loved us and then turned around and hurt us.

I want you to know that God's kind of love is different from anything else you have ever known. And only His supernatural love can heal you on the inside.

God adores you. He is deeply, deeply in love with you just the way you are *right now*, and He wants to have a personal relationship with you. Nevertheless, you need to understand what type of love He has to offer. In New Testament Greek, the authors used more than one word to talk specifically about distinct kinds of love. For example, the word *eros* refers to a sexual kind of love. And the word *philos* is the love in a friendship. Philadelphia, the "City of Brotherly Love," takes its name from a combination of *philos*, meaning "love," and *adelphos*, meaning "brother." The word *epithemi* means passion. If I say I love a sports team or love my car, I'm really saying I am passionate or enthusiastic about them. The word *storge* speaks to familial love, such as the love I have for my parents, brother, or sister. However, there's a unique word that speaks of God's love: *agape*. When God says He loves us, He is telling us that it is a love that is categorically different from all others. *Agape* is the only expression of love that doesn't require an emotion. Yes, God has emotion, but His love doesn't require it. When Jesus tells us to love our neighbors as ourselves, our emotions are not the driver. It doesn't matter how we feel about our neighbors. We do the right thing on their account regardless of the circumstances or how we feel about it, and that is *agape*.

God says, *"I will never leave you nor forsake you." So we may boldly say: "The Lord is my helper; I will not fear. What can man do to me?"* (Hebrews 13:6) God is making two promises to you right now: He will never leave you physically or spiritually, and He will never turn His heart away from you.

Throughout eternity, there will never be an instant when God turns His heart away from you.

He will forever and only do what's right for you. He will never betray you, reject you, or put you down.

In the past, people may have done some of those things to you. They might have said they loved you but followed it up with very hurtful words and actions. I promise you, God will never do that. I've been walking with the Lord for over 48 years, and I can tell you, without equivocation, that He is the most consistent and loving person I've ever known. I was a mess when I received Christ and His agape love picked me up where I was and has carried me from that point forward. And He will do the same for you. I want you to know and be sure that God is madly in love with you. He does not love you in the ways other people have done. You don't even have to sit and contemplate that possibility. Instead, get it into your heart and believe that it's true because that is the entire message of the Bible. He loves you with the highest, purest form of love.

HEALING FROM GOD'S WORD

Love has been perfected among us in this: that we may have boldness in the day of judgment; because as He is, so are we in this world. There is no fear in love; but perfect love casts out fear, because fear involves torment. But he who fears has not been made perfect in love. We love Him because He first loved us. (1 John 4:17–19)

Beloved, let us love one another, for love is of God; and everyone who loves is born of God and knows God. He who does not love does not know God, for God is love. In this the love of God was manifested toward us, that God has sent His only begotten Son into the world, that we might live through Him. In this is love, not that we loved God, but that He loved us and sent His Son to be the propitiation for our sins. Beloved, if God so loved us, we also ought to love one another. (1 John 4:7–11)

For God so loved the world that He gave His only begotten Son, that whoever believes in Him should not perish but have everlasting life. For God did not send His Son into the world to condemn the world, but that the world through Him might be saved. (John 3:16–17)

HEALING TRUTHS

- One of the greatest challenges you will face in your quest to fully believe in God's love is that most of the deepest hurts in your life often come from people who said they loved you and then rejected, betrayed, or abused you.

- The word "love" is a muddled and misused word in our culture. It is used to describe how we feel about everything and everyone in our lives, from our dogs to God, from our new pajamas to our parents, and from our sports teams to our spouses.

- God eternally promises us two things: First, He will never physically leave us. Second, He will never emotionally forsake us, which means He will never turn His heart away from us. That is the essence of agape love.

- We must be able to differentiate between human emotion and God's sacrificial and eternal commitment to us. When you understand the five distinct types of love found in the Bible, you will realize that many people in your life who told you they loved you and then hurt you may have had a positive emotion or attraction to you, but they didn't have God's love for you. God's agape love never changes and only does what is best for others.

- On your worst day, God is unwavering in His agape love for you. Regardless of the circumstances or how He feels, God will never change His mind or break His promises as others have done. He will *never, never, never* leave or forsake you. For the rest of eternity, your loving heavenly

Father will be with you, and His heart will be set on you. You cannot change that fact—it is eternally settled.

Exercises for Reflection and Discussion

1. Who are the people in your past or present who have told you they loved you but then hurt you? List them.

_____

_____

_____

_____

_____

_____

2. How have your experiences with these people affected your ability to trust others?

_____

_____

_____

_____

_____

_____

3. How do you believe the hurts people have caused you have affected your ability to trust God and believe in His love?

_____

_____

_____

_____

_____

_____

4. When you think about your prayer life and your other spiritual practices, how has a lack of trust in God affected them?

_____

_____

_____

_____

_____

_____

Applying Healing Principles

Complete the following steps to apply what you learned in the lesson:

1. **Forgive people on the list of those who hurt you.** I will be writing more in-depth about forgiveness later in this book, but for right now, take this opportunity to consider the people you need to forgive and prepare your heart to do it.

2. **Forgive yourself for mistakes you made in your relationships.** For example, you may have told someone that you love them, but then *you* hurt *them*. Or you may have been naive and opened your heart without wisdom to someone you should not have. You may have even been involved in sexual sin, an affair, an abortion, a betrayal, a divorce, or some other relationship mistake, and you regret it. You haven't forgiven yourself yet. Forgiving yourself is as important as forgiving others. Later in the book, I will discuss more about God's grace and how to overcome shame and condemnation.

3. **Trust in God's agape love.** Walk in an awareness of His presence with you and His love for you. Start simply by trusting that your prayers of faith will reveal more of God's promise of love. Trust in Him as you obey His Word and seek Him for guidance. Be at peace and have confidence as you trust in His goodness and in His ability to protect

and provide for you. As you grow in that trust, your overall disposition and attitude will change.

4. **Make a list of the things that upset or worry you.** Pray through your list and entrust those things to God. Ask the Lord to guide you, provide for you, protect you, and give you favor. As you pray, believe that He loves you and put your trust in Him.

Healing Confession

Confess the following aloud:
I confess, in agreement with God's Word, that God loves me with a sacrificial and eternal love. He will never leave me nor forsake me. Because of God's complete love for me, He is worthy of my total trust. I commit my life to loving Him and loving others with His type of love.

Healing Prayer

Silently or aloud, pray this prayer:
Loving Father, I pray that You will heal my heart from the wounds I have carried from my past or experienced in my present. I forgive every person who has done something to hurt me. I also ask You to forgive me for those I have hurt and mistakes I have made.

Holy Spirit, I pray You will fill me with God's agape love as You heal my mind and heart. I pray You will help me deal with every person and event in my life that has hurt me and damaged me. I pray You will remind me of things I have forgotten that I still need to address. I pray for You to totally heal my life, and as You do, I pray You will help me learn to trust and depend on You daily. I thank You that You are always with me and always care for me—when I am struggling and even in tough times. I thank You for Your incredible love for me. I accept it and believe it. In Jesus' name, amen.

Day 3

A God of Grace

If you want to experience inner healing, then you have to let the Holy Spirit repair your concept of God's grace. The Lord is good, even when you don't deserve His goodness. He loves you even when everyone else thinks you're unlovable. Even so, the devil works full-time to condemn you and convince you that God's acceptance of you is based on a point system. If you're doing well, then you may think you deserve God's favor. However, if you're not doing well, then you may think you don't deserve anything good.

You must understand that even on your absolute best day, there is nothing you can do to get God to respond with His favor. You don't deserve anything He does for you. *Everything* is based on grace.

Grace is unmerited favor. Grace is God loving you for no earthly reason, which means Heaven has an entirely different accounting system than we do. Grace means you receive what you don't deserve—and thank God, you don't receive what you do deserve. Jesus took your place on the cross and got what He didn't deserve, for which we also give thanks to God. He took the punishment for our sins. Jesus' death completely removed God's anger and the curse of sin in our lives if we will receive Jesus by faith. God is not mad at you, and it's not because of anything you did or didn't do. It's because of Jesus. It's all about grace.

Now, I want you to read this next set of verses carefully. Then read them again. Take some time to let them stir around in your heart and mind because they will bring healing to you.

But God, who is rich in mercy, because of His great love with which He loved us, even when we were dead in trespasses, made us alive together with Christ (by grace you have been saved), and raised us up together, and made us sit together in the heavenly places in Christ Jesus, that in the ages to come He might show the exceeding riches of His grace in His kindness toward us in Christ Jesus. For by grace you have been saved through faith, and that not of yourselves; it is the gift of God, not of works, lest anyone should boast. For we are His workmanship, created in Christ Jesus for good works, which God prepared beforehand that we should walk in them. (Ephesians 2:4–10)

Let this Scripture get inside you, then meditate on it, believe it, and confess it.

God, who is rich in mercy—your God and your Father—is deeply, madly in love with you.

His mercy and grace mean you don't get what you deserve. Understand you don't deserve anything good, but He is so rich in mercy and grace that He is going to give good things to you anyway. And all these things come directly from God's Word.

My father was emotionally distant. I grew up in a performance-based home, which led me to judge every relationship in my life on a point system. If someone did well, then I liked them better. But if they didn't do well, then I didn't like them so well. But God's relationship with us isn't performance-based. Do you realize that when you need God the most, you deserve Him the least? It is also then that the devil starts talking the loudest to us. He says, "Don't bother even trying to talk to God right now. You must get your act together before you pray because He won't even listen to you. In fact, you're a great disappointment to God. You've done all these things wrong, and you need to get your act together before you pray."

The writer of Hebrews says, *"Let us therefore come boldly to the throne of grace, that we may obtain mercy and find grace to help in time of need"* (Hebrews 4:16). In the previous verse, he writes, *"For we do not have a High Priest who cannot sympathize with our weaknesses, but was in all* points *tempted as* we are, yet *without sin"* (Hebrews 4:15). Our God has been to earth in human flesh, and He faced all the temptations we have experienced, underwent the same sufferings. He knew rejection. He felt pain.

When you approach Jesus for help, know that you're dealing with your best friend, who understands everything you've been through because He's experienced it too, though He never sinned. He understands every temptation you have experienced or will ever face. Those moments are when you need His grace because without it, you won't be able to approach God. With it, you can go to Him because He loves you so much. God accepts you just the way you are. Because of what Jesus has done, you can go to God and say, "Lord, I'm really hurting and struggling. I know I shouldn't have said or done those things. Please help me." God will not respond to you with legalism or judgment. He won't tell you that you make Him sick, or He's tired of you. If that is what you hear, then that message didn't come from God; those are the things the devil says.

God is on your side.

When you are struggling, go to your friend and approach the throne of grace.

He is the only one who can get you past whatever it is you're going through. Let God show you His love and acceptance. His power is what makes you able to process issues from your past so you can be healed. Because of Jesus, God will bless you, even though you don't deserve it, freely, without merit, and as a gift of grace.

HEALING FROM GOD'S WORD

Seeing then that we have a great High Priest who has passed through the heavens, Jesus the Son of God, let us hold fast our confession. For we do not have a High Priest who cannot sympathize with our weaknesses, but was in all points tempted as we are, yet without sin. Let us therefore come boldly to the throne of grace, that we may obtain mercy and find grace to help in time of need. (Hebrews 4:14–16)

But God, who is rich in mercy, because of His great love with which He loved us, even when we were dead in trespasses, made us alive together with Christ (by grace you have been saved), and raised us up together, and made us sit together in the heavenly places in Christ Jesus, that in the ages to come He might show the exceeding riches of His grace in His kindness toward us in Christ Jesus. For by grace you have been saved through faith, and that not of yourselves; it is the gift of God, not of works, lest anyone should boast. (Ephesians 2:4–9)

What then shall we say to these things? If God is for us, who can be against us? He who did not spare His own Son, but delivered Him up for us all, how shall He not with Him also freely give us all things? Who shall bring a charge against God's elect? It is God who justifies. Who is he who condemns? It is Christ who died, and furthermore is also risen, who is even at the right hand of God, who also makes intercession for us. Who shall separate us from the love of Christ? Shall tribulation, or distress, or persecution, or famine, or nakedness, or peril, or sword? As it is written: "For Your sake we are killed all day long; We are accounted as sheep for the slaughter." Yet in all these things we are more than conquerors through Him who loved us. For I am persuaded that neither death nor life, nor angels nor principalities nor powers, nor things present nor things to come, nor height nor depth, nor any other created thing, shall be able to separate us from the love of God which is in Christ Jesus our Lord. (Romans 8:31–39)

HEALING TRUTHS

- You will never be able to deserve anything God does for you. You don't deserve for Him to save, forgive, or bless you. You don't deserve for Him to love you or allow you to spend eternity in Heaven with Him. Everything God does for you, He does by grace because He loves you.

- God does not relate to you based on your performance or on any kind of point system. Even though God blesses us when we obey Him and put our faith in Him, He doesn't love us more. And just like any good father, God at times disciplines us for our good. But it doesn't mean He loves us less. It actually means the opposite. His discipline means He receives us as His child and cares for us too much to allow us to harm ourselves and others. (Read Hebrews 12:3-13) You can't earn God's love, and you don't have to. His accounting system is all based on His mercy, grace, and love.

- Many hurts in your life stem from old or recent performance-based relationships. Those relationships produced anxiety, fear, rejection, comparison, and insecurity. You live in a perpetual state of feeling you must deserve everything you get.

- You need God the most in the everyday struggles of life, when you wrestle with sin, when you feel discouraged, when you face financial problems, when you deal with difficult people, and when you want to break out of unhealthy cycles with harmful habits and addictions—but those are the times when you deserve Him the least.

- God is the most gracious person you will ever know. It is such a blessing to know that in that grace-based relationship, God totally loves you, and He won't reject you.

Exercises for Reflection and Discussion

1. Who has rejected you because you didn't measure up to their expectations? Make a list. The deepest hurts in our lives come from rejection. We must name those who rejected us, forgive them, and realize they don't represent God in any way.

_____

_____

_____

_____

_____

_____

2. Do you require others to perform in order to deserve your love or goodwill? Why or why not?

_____

_____

_____

_____

_____

_____

_____

3. Do you think of yourself as a gracious and merciful person? Why or why not?

_____

_____

_____

_____

_____

4. Is it difficult for you to receive something you feel you haven't earned and don't deserve? Why or why not?

_____

_____

_____

_____

_____

_____

5. What is the greatest barrier blocking you from believing in and receiving God's grace?

_____

_____

_____

_____

_____

_____

Applying Healing Principles

Complete the following steps to apply what you have learned in the lesson:

1. **Forgive those who have rejected you and made you perform to receive their love.**

2. **Meditate on Ephesians 2:4–9 and pray for the Holy Spirit to use those verses to minister the truth of God's love, mercy, and grace to your spirit.** Read that passage of Scripture often as the Holy Spirit is healing you of perfor-

mance-based love. The Holy Spirit is the Spirit of Truth, and He will use the Bible to heal you, minister truth to you, and deliver you from the lies that have harmed you.

3. **Offer your prayers to God with a new sense of boldness and confidence in His grace and mercy.** This type of praying is especially important when you are struggling and know you don't deserve God's love or grace. You can even begin your prayers by saying something like the following:

Father, I realize I don't deserve Your love and help right now—and I praise You that I don't have to. I come to You by the grace You provided for me by the blood of Jesus. I thank You for Your grace and mercy, and right now, I need help with _____. In Jesus' name, amen.

Healing Confession

Confess the following aloud:
I stand in agreement with God's Word as I confess that God's grace has saved me and not because I have earned it. Everything He has done or will ever do in my life is because He is rich in mercy and has great love for me. God made me special in my mother's womb. I am His child, and that is why He loves me. God loves me despite my sins and struggles, and I can only overcome my problems by going to His throne of grace for mercy

and help when I need it the most and deserve it the least.

Healing Prayer

Silently or aloud, pray this prayer:
Gracious Father, I thank You for Your mercy and grace for me. I thank You that I don't have to deserve Your love. Performance-based love and rejection from other people have hurt me deeply. I pray You will heal me of those hurts. I pray You will also heal me of my tendency to relate to others based on their performance. I want You to heal me by Your grace so I can relate to You and those around me by grace.

Holy Spirit, I invite You to fill me right now with God's love and power. I ask You to teach me how to relate to God and others by grace and to transform areas of my life that need to change. In Jesus' name, amen.

FINAL THOUGHTS ON SECTION ONE
Letting God Be God

The greatest need all of us have in our lives is to *receive love.* Our greatest fear is *rejection.* Think about your most painful inner wounds. Isn't it true that most of them come from rejection? We often encounter people who only accept us conditionally, and they change how we view ourselves. They say words and take actions that wound us, and some of them are our closest family members and loved ones. And maybe they do really love us, but they don't understand the pain they cause. However, you need to understand that God's love is categorically different from everyone else's. You can open your heart to Him with no fear. The apostle John reminds us that God's perfect love casts out our fear, including the fear of rejection, punishment, or of someone finding out the truth about what's inside of you.

People do love us, but their love is often based on what they don't know about us because if they really knew, they might change their minds about loving us. Nevertheless, God knows every detail of your life, inside and out. He knows what you do, think, and every other thing you'll ever think or do. God isn't ignorant about any area of your life. He has perfect knowledge about you, yet He loves you all the same and more than anyone else. That understanding of His love is what heals our hearts. When you allow His love on the inside of you, and you believe it by faith, then healing can grow.

Will you allow God to heal you? Then remember what the psalmist wrote: *"He sent His word and healed them, And delivered them from their destructions"* (Psalm 107:20). God's Word has brought dramatic inner healing to mine and Karen's lives. The writer of Hebrews reminds us just how powerful the

Word of God is: *"For the word of God is living and powerful, and sharper than any two-edged sword, piercing even to the division of soul and spirit, and of joints and marrow, and is a discerner of the thoughts and intents of the heart"* (Hebrews 4:12). The Scriptures are like a surgeon's scalpel, which can go inside of us and fix our broken parts.

So read Psalm 107:20 repeatedly until it takes root in your heart and heals you. As you meditate on it, confess the truth, and God will begin to do a deep healing work in your heart. With each lesson you read, let the inner healing process continue. As I end this section, let me remind you again: God is a good God, He loves you, He's for you, He's on your side, and He's a perfect Father. He's totally in love with you, and He wants to heal you. You can trust Him with the innermost parts of your heart. He will not harm you, betray you, let you down, or reject you. When you come to Him, you will walk into the gentle hands of the most loving Being in the universe.

SECTION TWO

OUR HEALER: THE HOLY SPIRIT

If we want inner health, one of the most important things for us to understand is that the Holy Spirit is our healer. He is God and a co-equal member of the Trinity—Father, Son, and *Holy Spirit*.

Day 4

The Promise of the Helper

Jesus went to the Jordan River to be water baptized by John the Baptist. As Jesus came out of the water, the Holy Spirit descended on Him like a dove, and God the Father said, *"This is My beloved Son, in whom I am well pleased"* (Matthew 3:17). Jesus always operated under the power of the Spirit. When He was preparing His disciples for the time He would go back to heaven, He said, *"These things I have spoken to you while being present with you. But the Helper, the Holy Spirit, whom the Father will send in My name, He will teach you all things, and bring to your remembrance all things that I said to you"* (John 14:25–26).

In fact, Jesus told His followers that it would be better off for Him to go away because when He did, He would send the Holy Spirit to be with them. That is exactly what happened on the day of Pentecost. The Holy Spirit fell upon the whole church, and all of us whom Jesus has saved also have the Holy Spirit. However, that doesn't mean we have the same relationship with Him that we need, and He wants us to have. We have access to unlimited healing power, but we often limp along as though we are helpless.

When writing about the Holy Spirit, the apostle Paul said, *"The fruit of the Spirit is love, joy, peace, patience, kindness, goodness, faithfulness, gentleness, [and] self-control"* (Galatians 5:22, NASB). Take all those emotional qualities together and you have the personality and character of God. Paul says those who are under the control of the Holy Spirit also have those qualities—that is the fruit of the Spirit. The fruit is available, but we don't always take advantage of it.

———

You see, God designed the engine of your emotions to run with the oil of the Holy Spirit.

———

When Paul wrote about the fruit of the Spirit, he also warned the Galatians about the deeds of the flesh, which means our fallen nature. Paul says that outbursts of anger, jealousy, envy, and all those kinds of actions cause us to overheat like an engine that doesn't have oil. This causes friction overload, and then we lock down. God never designed us to run without the Holy Spirit.

When we invite the Holy Spirit to take control of our emotions every day, we say, "Holy Spirit, I need you today. I'm hurting. There are some people who have said things to me, and there are people who have done things to me. I'm having these feelings. I want to respond in anger to this person. I've got issues with other people I'm going to have to deal with today. Holy Spirit, take charge of my life, and I invite you to come in and give me the fruit of the Spirit. I want the oil of the Holy Spirit to help me manage my emotions." I have been a believer a long time, and I can just tell you, it makes a dramatic difference every day when I invite the Holy Spirit to take control. Jesus called the Spirit our Helper and told us He would send the Holy Spirit to us (see John 14:15–31). Bible translators derive the word "helper" from the Greek word *paraclatos* (or *paraclete*), and it means someone who will walk with you and help you. That is exactly what the Holy Spirit does for us. He's on the inside of us as our Helper. Emotionally, I can't be the person I'm supposed to be without help from the Holy Spirit. In fact, I wouldn't even try it.

At Creation, when God made Adam, He breathed life into Adam's nostrils. God didn't simply deliver oxygen to Adam's lungs; He breathed His Spirit into Adam. As a result, when Adam and Eve sinned, the Holy Spirit left them. We are now under a New Covenant, which Jesus Christ sealed by His own blood on the cross. He will never leave us nor forsake us, so the Holy Spirit will never leave us because He is in us if we are believers. In fact, the Holy Spirit is in you right now if Jesus has saved you. What I want for you is that you would acknowledge the presence of the Holy Spirit in your life. I want you to begin now to have a daily, dependent relationship with the Holy Spirit. My hope is that you will learn to depend on the Holy Spirit so that you will talk to Him and invite Him to come in and heal you on the inside and give you new strength.

HEALING FROM GOD'S WORD

But when the Helper comes, whom I shall send to you from the Father, the Spirit of truth who proceeds from the Father, He will testify of Me. (John 15:26)

Nevertheless I tell you the truth. It is to your advantage that I go away; for if I do not go away, the Helper will not come to you; but if I depart, I will send Him to you. (John 16:7)

I still have many things to say to you, but you cannot bear them now. However, when He, the Spirit of truth, has come, He will guide you into all truth; for He will not speak on His own authority, but whatever He hears He will speak; and He will tell you things to come. He will glorify Me, for He will take of what is Mine and declare it to you. All things that the Father has are Mine. Therefore I said that He will take of Mine and declare it to you. (John 16:12–15)

For those who live according to the flesh set their minds on the things of the flesh, but those who live according to the Spirit, the things of the Spirit. For to be carnally minded is death, but to be spiritually minded is life and peace. Because the carnal mind is enmity against God; for it is not subject to the law of God, nor indeed can be.

So then, those who are in the flesh cannot please God.
(Romans 8:5–8)

HEALING TRUTHS

- The Holy Spirit isn't an "it." He is a person, and He is God. He is the third person of the Godhead—Father, Son, and *Holy Spirit*. We don't worship three gods; we have one God manifested in three persons.

- The three persons of the Godhead are co-existent, co-equal, and co-eternal. Each person of the Godhead fulfills a special role in our salvation and daily lives.

- Jesus identifies the Holy Spirit by the name "Helper." Paraclete, the word translated "Helper" from Greek, means someone called to walk beside and help, which is precisely what the Holy Spirit does. The presence of the Holy Spirit in our lives manifests all the benefits of salvation Jesus died to give us.

- The Holy Spirit is always gentle and gracious. He is the kindest person you will ever know, but He is also the most powerful being in the Universe—He is God.

- God did not design us for our emotions to operate separately from the Holy Spirit. He is oil to the engine of our emotions. As an engine cannot run without oil, we will also overheat emotionally and suffer damage if we try to function without the Holy Spirit. As we depend on Him, we "hum" right along without overheating or doing damage to ourselves and others.

- God created us in His image. As such, we simply cannot function emotionally if we do not depend on the Holy Spirit every day. His presence is what will heal the damage from our past as He coats our emotions with love, joy, peace, patience, kindness, goodness, faithfulness, gentleness, and self-control.

Exercises for Reflection and Discussion

1. How much would you say you think about God's presence every day? How do you feel about the answer you gave?

_____

_____

_____

_____

_____

_____

2. How often would you say you pray and ask the Holy Spirit to give you help with your emotions?

_____

_____

_____

_____

_____

_____

3. Do you see dependence upon God as a sign of strength or weakness? Why did you give the answer you did?

_____

_____

_____

_____

_____

_____

4. How would you describe your relationship with the Holy Spirit?

_____

_____

_____

_____

_____

_____

Applying Healing Principles

Complete the following steps to apply what you have learned in the lesson:

1. **Ask the Holy Spirit to fill you with His presence.** Just as you received Jesus by faith in God's grace, do the same with the Holy Spirit. He is present in your life from the moment Jesus saves you, but the specific manifestations of the Spirit's presence occur as you invite Him to do His work in your life and acknowledge your dependence on Him.

2. **Be specific with the Holy Spirit as you pray for emotional healing.** From the lists you made in the previous lesson, pray specifically about the people who have hurt you the most and the issues that caused you the most damage. As you pray, ask the Holy Spirit to heal you and to give you God's supernatural emotional power.

3. **Treat the Holy Spirit as a person.** Talk to Him and express your love with praise, worship, and words of affection.

49

Listen to the Holy Spirit because He is an expert at communicating through words and other impressions and expressions. Remember, His voice will always be consistent with the Bible and the character of Christ.

Healing Confession

Confess the following aloud:
In agreement with God's Word, I confess that the Holy Spirit is my Helper. Jesus sent Him to me as a gift of grace to help me in every area of my life. The Holy Spirit is with me now to empower me, to lead me into all truth, to remind me of Jesus, and to give me the emotional grace to accept Your healing and supernatural emotional health. From this day forward, I commit that I will live in dependence upon the Holy Spirit. This is how God designed me to live, and it is the secret to living a victorious life in Christ.

Healing Prayer

Silently or aloud, pray this prayer:
Holy Spirit, I receive You into my life as God by faith as a gift of grace. I don't deserve You, but I receive You as a gift. I cherish Your presence in my life, and from this day forward, I commit that I will depend on You for power, guidance, and emotional strength. I ask You to minister complete emotional healing in

my life as only You can do. Give me the manifestation of the fruit of the Spirit in my life. I cannot love people or live my life as I should without Your help. I will rely on You every day to give me the emotional grace to love others and relate to them by Your power. In Jesus' name, amen!

Day 5

The Spirit and Your Flesh

When we speak of the Holy Spirit, we need to know the part of us that is not of the Spirit: our flesh, which is our fallen nature. We must understand how God made us and what happened because of Adam and Eve's sin. God made them in His image to live in His presence. He breathed His own life into them, which gave them provisional immortality, meaning they would not be immortal apart from Him. If they had not sinned, Adam and Eve would still be alive today, but they *did* sin. And when they did, they fell out of relationship with God and caused the entire human race to fall with them. They took their fallen nature after they sinned and passed it down to all of us. That is the reason no one is born saved. Every person must receive Christ individually, and all humans have a fallen nature that will be with them for the rest of their lives, even if they do become saved.

Those of us alive on earth still have our flesh, which is the carnal or natural part of us. It is the part of us that doesn't act like God, doesn't want Him, and resists Him. Speaking about the struggle of our flesh against the Holy Spirit, the apostle Paul told the Galatians:

I say then: Walk in the Spirit, and you shall not fulfill the lust of the flesh. For the flesh lusts against the Spirit, and the Spirit against the flesh; and these are contrary to one another, so that you do not do the things that you wish. But if you are led by the Spirit, you are not under the law.

Now the works of the flesh are evident, which are: adultery, fornication, uncleanness, lewdness, idolatry, sorcery, hatred, contentions, jealousies, outbursts of wrath, selfish ambitions, dissensions, heresies, envy, murders, drunkenness, revelries, and the like; of which I tell you beforehand, just as I also told you in time past, that those who practice such things will not inherit the kingdom of God.

But the fruit of the Spirit is love, joy, peace, long-suffering, kindness, goodness, faithfulness, gentleness, self-control. Against such there is no law. And those who are Christ's have crucified the flesh with its passions and desires. If we live in the Spirit, let us also walk in the Spirit. Let us not become conceited, provoking one another, envying one another. (Galatians 5:16–26)

Here is an important concept you must understand about the battle between the flesh and the Spirit: this is a *daily* decision. I've known Christ for many years, but I didn't always know this. It took a long time for me to understand that I'm still walking in the flesh more times than I care to admit. I can wake up one day and be carnal. I can be hateful or short-tempered. Sometimes I am jealous or envious. All those reactions happen when my flesh takes over. All the deeds of the flesh Paul lists are our natural, default setting if we are not believers or when we aren't depending on Christ.

Every day, I must consciously choose to let the Holy Spirit take control so I can be healed and be the person God wants me to be.

You only have two choices: either walk by the Holy Spirit or walk by the flesh. However, your fallen flesh will be with you for the rest of your life in this world. Paul wrote to the Romans, *"For the good that I will to do, I do not do; but the evil I will not to do, that I practice. Now if I do what I will not to do, it is no longer I who do it, but sin that dwells in me"* (Romans 7:19–20). I can relate to these verses, and I am sure you can too. We can try all we want with our own willpower, but we cannot achieve goodness on our own.

We do become frustrated when we fail. You may try to be a good person, but then you're not, and it's overwhelming. But Paul did not leave the Christians in Rome with no hope, and you can have that same hope. He cries out in despair, *"O wretched man that I am! Who will deliver me from this body of death?"* (Romans 7:24). If Paul had finished his letter there, it would have been very discouraging when the church in Rome received it, but that is not where it ends. In the very next verse, he declares the answer: *"I thank God—through Jesus Christ our Lord!"* (v.25) And then, for the entire next chapter, Paul tells the Roman believers just how much they can count on the victory they have received in Jesus and through the power of the Holy Spirit. He mentions the Holy Spirit fifteen times in the first sixteen verses. He is letting the Christians in Rome know the same thing he told the Christians in Galatia—the answer to your flesh is the Holy Spirit. So here in Romans chapter 8, Paul says the Holy Spirit delivers us from the predicament we have with the flesh. God designed you to operate under the power of the Holy Spirit, and that is what I want for you. I want you to let Him come in and help you overcome the deeds of your flesh.

HEALING FROM GOD'S WORD

For what I am doing, I do not understand. For what I will to do, that I do not practice; but what I hate, that I do. If, then, I do what I will not to do, I agree with the law that it is good. But now, it is no longer I who do it, but sin that dwells in me. For I know that in me (that is, in my flesh) nothing good dwells; for to will is present with me, but how to perform what is good I do not find. For the good that I will to do, I do not do; but the evil I will not to do, that I practice. Now if I do what I will not to do, it is no longer I who do it, but sin that dwells in me.

I find then a law, that evil is present with me, the one who wills to do good. For I delight in the law of God according to the inward man. But I see another law in my members, warring against the law of my mind, and bringing me into captivity to the law of sin which is in my members. O wretched man that I am! Who will deliver me from this body of death? I thank God—through Jesus Christ our Lord!

So then, with the mind I myself serve the law of God, but with the flesh the law of sin.

There is therefore now no condemnation to those who are in Christ Jesus, who do not walk according to the flesh, but according to the Spirit. For the law of the Spirit of life in Christ Jesus has made me free from the law of sin and death. For what the law could not do in that it was weak through the flesh, God did by sending His own Son in the likeness of sinful flesh, on account of sin: He condemned sin in the flesh, that the righteous requirement of the law might be fulfilled in us who do not walk according to the flesh but according to the Spirit. For those who live according to the flesh set their minds on the things of the flesh, but those who live according to the Spirit, the things of the Spirit. For to be carnally minded is death, but to be spiritually minded is life and peace. Because the carnal mind is enmity against God;

for it is not subject to the law of God, nor indeed can be. So then, those who are in the flesh cannot please God.

But you are not in the flesh but in the Spirit, if indeed the Spirit of God dwells in you. Now if anyone does not have the Spirit of Christ, he is not His. And if Christ is in you, the body is dead because of sin, but the Spirit is life because of righteousness. But if the Spirit of Him who raised Jesus from the dead dwells in you, He who raised Christ from the dead will also give life to your mortal bodies through His Spirit who dwells in you.

Therefore, brethren, we are debtors—not to the flesh, to live according to the flesh. For if you live according to the flesh you will die; but if by the Spirit you put to death the deeds of the body, you will live. (Romans 7:15–8:13)

I say then: Walk in the Spirit, and you shall not fulfill the lust of the flesh. For the flesh lusts against the Spirit, and the Spirit against the flesh; and these are contrary to one another, so that you do not do the things that you wish. But if you are led by the Spirit, you are not under the law. Now the works of the flesh are evident, which are: adultery, fornication, uncleanness, lewdness, idolatry, sorcery, hatred, contentions, jealousies, outbursts of wrath, selfish ambitions, dissensions, heresies, envy, murders, drunkenness, revelries, and the like; of which I tell you beforehand, just as I also told you in time past, that those who practice such things will not inherit the kingdom of God. But the fruit of the Spirit is love, joy, peace, longsuffering, kindness, goodness, faithfulness, gentleness, self-control. Against such there is no law. (Galatians 5:16–23)

HEALING TRUTHS

- The Holy Spirit's archnemesis is our flesh, which is our fallen nature. According to God's Word, you have only two choices each day about what will drive you: your flesh (fallen nature) or the Holy Spirit.

- Although God loves all of us, no one is born saved. We are all born spiritually dead with fallen natures—our flesh. The reality of our fallen nature began to manifest very soon after we took our first breaths. We are naturally selfish, rebellious, and against healthy community.

- Our Helper, the Holy Spirit, empowers us to live through His presence in our lives. He makes us victorious sons and daughters of God. Everything Adam and Eve lost through their sin, Jesus has restored to us, and even more. You receive these things by God's grace as a gift when you put your faith in the blood of Jesus.

- Although Jesus forgave and filled you with the Holy

Spirit, your flesh or fallen nature is still fully alive and will constantly be with you either until you die and go to Heaven or Jesus returns and takes you in the rapture of the Church. No one is an exception to this truth.

- Every day, as you wake up, your natural default setting will be to live by the power of your flesh or fallen nature. You must also understand that people who live that way hurt and damage others emotionally.

- You have only one answer to how you can overcome your flesh, and that is the Holy Spirit. According to the apostle Paul, you can either live under the influence of your fallen flesh or under the influence of the Holy Spirit. There isn't a third choice.

- If you are going to be healed and healthy, then you must understand the nature of your flesh and its negative potential in your life every day. Every morning when you wake up, you must actively reject the default of your fallen flesh and choose to walk by the Spirit. You must acknowledge the Holy Spirit's presence in your life, remain aware of your sin nature, and ask Him for help, both generally and specifically, for each challenge you will face.

Exercises for Reflection and Discussion

1. What are the main ways your flesh manifests itself daily? What are your primary struggles with sin?

_____

_____

_____

_____

_____

_____

2. What wounds have been created in your life because of the fleshly behavior of others?

_____

_____

_____

_____

_____

_____

3. As you consider fleshly behavior, do certain people come to your mind? Make a list.

_____

_____

_____

_____

_____

_____

4. What are some of the ways you have tried to change your negative behavior but then failed instead?

_____

_____

_____

_____

_____

_____

Applying Healing Principles

Complete the following steps to apply what you have learned in the lesson:

1. **Acknowledge the constant presence of your fleshly nature to the Holy Spirit, and then ask Him to fill you with His power and nature.** The wonderful thing about the Holy Spirit is when you trust Him and ask Him for help, He will change your desires and abilities. Without Him, you will keep desiring the wrong things and feel powerless to change. Notice that one trait of the fruit of the Holy Spirit is self-control. With Him, your desires change, and He gives you the power to do what you need to do.

2. **Form a daily habit of changing the default setting of your life from your flesh to the Holy Spirit.** Every day, you have to make this choice—sometimes several times per day. Be especially aware when you are under stress or going through some difficulty. It is then that you must decide to depend on the Holy Spirit rather than react according to your flesh.

3. **Think about and meditate on the presence of the Holy Spirit in your life often.** In this way, you will walk in the presence of God.

Healing Confession

Confess the following aloud:

I agree and confess, according to God's Word, that I have a fallen nature within me, which is both sinful and selfish. I know I was born in a fallen state, and the default setting in my life is to live according to my flesh. The only solution to this problem is for me to have a daily reliance on the power of the Holy Spirit. He alone can give me the strength and ability to overcome my flesh as He supernaturally changes my desires and abilities. As a gift of grace, the Holy Spirit will help me in my weakness when I need Him most and deserve Him the least. In the sins and struggles of my life, He is with me to help me overcome and to live as God intended me to do.

Healing Prayer

Silently or aloud, pray this prayer:

Holy Spirit, I admit to You that I have a fallen flesh that wants to rebel against God and His commandments. I admit that I have sinned and will continue to want to sin to the degree that I allow my flesh to control my life. The only solution for me is to rely on You and to walk with a moment-by-moment awareness of Your presence and power in my life. I ask You to fill me with Your power and love and for You to change my desires to Your desires and give me the power to change. I will not offer this prayer only one time—this is a new daily prayer for me. I acknowledge that my willpower isn't the answer to my problems. Your power is the only answer. I choose to no longer allow my flesh to control my life. I turn my life over to Your power. Beginning this very moment, I crucify my flesh and put it to death. As I take this step, I turn to You and pray for Your power, life, and love to fill me as You manifest the fruit of the Spirit in my life. Give me the power to live and love according to the nature and character of Jesus. In His name, amen.

FINAL THOUGHTS ON SECTION TWO

The Spirit Inside Us

I know there are some things inside you that need healing. You might have some unforgiveness or anger. You may have some deep wounds that fuel your flesh. You need the Holy Spirit to heal you. I want you to understand from this day forward that the solution to your flesh isn't more effort or willpower. The answer is His power. The Holy Spirit is the one who can give you the ability to act, think, and feel the way God wants you to do. You need Him to do an important work in you, and you need it to begin today.

Jesus sent the Holy Spirit to live with us, to be in us for eternity. God is with us by His Spirit. He is the same Spirit who hovered over the deep when God created the universe, the same Spirit who hovered over Mary and placed the infant Jesus inside her, and the same Spirit who raised Jesus from the dead. He is now the same Holy Spirit who lives inside you. He loves you, adores you, and will never leave you. He is the only one who has the power to do what needs to be done inside you. The Holy Spirit is the oil in the engine of your emotions who can keep you from destroying yourself on the inside. Don't count on your willpower; rely on His power. It's not your character or personality that will turn your life around; God's character and personality are what will set you free. His Holy Spirit will do surgery in your heart, healing you from the inside out.

Your flesh desires to act against God, but you can't change on your own to become a better person. You can only change how much you will depend on the Holy Spirit. Every day when you awake, acknowledge,

Lord, I've got flesh, and it wants to do and say some things that are wrong. I want you to change my desires. I don't want to live the rest of my life trying not to do something my flesh really wants to do. I need your help to transform my desires. I want you to change me from the inside out. Do surgery on all my hurts. I give you permission to take anything out of me that does not belong. And I want you to give me the ability to talk, act, and relate to others the way I should. Change me from being a worldly person into a godly person. Heal me from the inside out. In Jesus' name, amen.

SECTION THREE

———

ENTER THE ADVERSARY

Someone wants to destroy your life.

He wants the worst for you, and he has been trying to work in your life for years. You might not even know that he is up to this activity, but I am going to uncover him for you.

We call him the diabolos, the devil.

Day 6

O Diabolos, The Slanderer

This is what the Apostle Paul wrote to the believers in Ephesus: *"'Be angry, and do not sin:' do not let the sun go down on your wrath, nor give place to the devil"* (Ephesians 4:26). Paul says that all of us get angry—and that's okay—but don't go to sleep holding it or using it as an excuse to sin. The danger of going to bed on anger is that it gives place to the devil. The Greek word for "devil" in Ephesians 4:26 is the word "diabolos" and it means "slanderer". The truth that the Apostle Paul is trying to convey to us is that when we don't process our anger in a timely manner and get it out of us, it gives the devil access to our thoughts and emotions and he uses that opportunity to slander the one we are angry with. The devil is a master slanderer and only God knows how many relationships he has destroyed and the lives he has broken through his lies.

I may shock you when I say this, but if you've gone to bed holding onto anger, then you've been counseled by the devil whether you know it or not. Your memories are like a house. Have you ever noticed in your own home that the rooms in which you spend the most time are also the rooms you change the most? You probably haven't changed the furniture in a rarely used guest room for several years, but your living room changes more often. The same is true with your memories when you hold anger and bitterness. You think about events that have happened and rehearse hurts and offenses over and over again. The more you spend time in that "room," the worse the memories become. It's not an upgrade, but it is certainly a change. Why does this happen? It is because the devil wants to shape your memories in a way that will cause more anger and division. He is a master slanderer.

I am the first to admit that early in our marriage, I used to fight with my wife. Karen and I would get into an argument, and I was the kind of person who would go to bed angry. I would become quiet and ruminate, then I would become a browbeater. But I remember laying in bed one night with all these thoughts racing through my mind. Some of those thoughts were mine, but then some of them weren't mine at all because I can remember when the devil, *diabolos*, would try to speak to me. At the time, I didn't know it was him because he's very clever at hiding and disguising his words as our own thoughts. As a result, I would have terrible thoughts in my anger, but the devil was really the author of many of them.

In the Garden of Eden, the devil took the form of a serpent. He loves that form because it fits his character, both danger-ous and stealthy. You often don't know a serpent is there until it strikes, just like the devil. Concealed, he's there, trying to help you remodel the room.

About halfway through Jesus' ministry, He told his disciples He would die on a cross. Peter at once rebuked Him. Jesus turned to Peter and said, *"Get behind me, Satan"* (see Matthew 16:21–23, my paraphrase). Jesus didn't think Peter was actually the devil—He recognized devil-talk coming out of his friend's mouth. Satan introduced thoughts into Peter's mind, and Peter didn't even know it. But Jesus knew.

I want you to understand that the devil can access your negative emotions when you don't manage them correctly. When someone hurt you in the past, you became angry. But if you get hurt and don't forgive that person, then you choose to let bitterness stew inside of you, and it opens a door for the devil. He walks right through that door and uses it as an opportunity to slander someone to you. He speaks bitterness into your heart and even reconstructs your memories to make the offense worse than it really was.

Often, you won't even know it's the devil you're dealing with, but I want you to recognize how you can know. In the next steps we take together, I want you to think about those people who have hurt you. Consider whether you've forgiven those people. Next, I want you to ask yourself if your beliefs about those people were put there by the devil? All of us, when we have negative emotions that we haven't managed properly, open ourselves up for the devil to insert slanderous thoughts and accuse people to us because he hates healthy relationships. He doesn't want you to have a happy marriage, godly friendships, or a positive work environment. The devil doesn't want you to be happy at all. He only comes to steal, kill, and destroy (see John 10:10). How does he do those things? The same way he did it to Adam and Eve. He will slither into your life, speak lies that cause you to divide your relationships with God and others, and then he will slither out and leave you devastated.

Some of your hurts, pain, and problems happened because you or someone else believed untrue things the devil put in your minds .

He changed the room on you. We're going to uncover *diabolos* today, and we're going to learn how to undo the damage he's done by the power of the Holy Spirit.

HEALING FROM GOD'S WORD

Who is wise and understanding among you? Let him show by good conduct that his works are done in the meekness of wisdom. But if you have bitter envy and self-seeking in your hearts, do not boast and lie against the truth. This wisdom does not descend from above, but is earthly, sensual, demonic. For where envy and self-seeking exist, confusion and every evil thing are there. But the wisdom that is from above is first pure, then peaceable, gentle, willing to yield, full of mercy and good fruits, without partiality and without hypocrisy. (James 3:13–17)

For God has not given us a spirit of fear, but of power and of love and of a sound mind. (2 Timothy 1:7)

Let no corrupt word proceed out of your mouth, but what is good for necessary edification, that it may impart grace to the hearers. And do not grieve the Holy Spirit of God, by whom you were sealed for the day of redemption. Let all bitterness, wrath, anger, clamor, and evil speaking be put away from you, with all malice. And be kind to one another, tenderhearted, forgiving one another, even as God in Christ forgave you. (Ephesians 4:29–32)

"Be angry, and do not sin": do not let the sun go down on your wrath, nor give place to the devil. (Ephesians 4:26–27)

HEALING TRUTHS

- One of the most troubling realities is that the devil has access to our negative emotions when we nurse them and don't deal with them properly. If you harbor anger long-term, then you give the devil a foothold into your life. He uses that open door to accuse and slander the person against whom you hold a grudge, which includes your spouse, parents, a friend, a boss, and others. He will even remodel our memories to make them worse than they really were. The devil's aim is to divide us!

- If you have gone to sleep angry at someone, then you have been counseled by the devil, even if you don't know it. You must understand when you have toxic emotions within you that they are open doors for demonic intrusion.

- World history contains many examples of the devil accusing and slandering God to humanity and humans to each other. The devil wants to keep us devastated and divided. He does all of this by accessing your fallen emotions and introducing negative, divisive, and unbiblical thoughts into your mind. The most crucial step for you to take to stop the devil from getting to your emotions is first to understand how he works.

- The devil doesn't want you to know he engages in your thoughts, emotions, or relationships. He simply wants you to think you are dealing with people who are odd, difficult, or evil, but that is a lie. The devil is your real enemy, and he wants to destroy every good thing in your life.

- Not only does the devil use anger to slander and accuse

God and others, but he wants to get you to accuse your-self. He is an expert at using toxic emotions to destroy your self-esteem and feelings of hope for the future. The devil will try to convince you that God doesn't love you or even like you. He wants you to see yourself as a loser. His goal is to drive you into isolation and hopelessness.

- If you have harbored negative emotions for a long time, then you have thoughts in your mind about God, people, and yourself that aren't true. God wants to free you from the devil's tyrannical assaults upon your mind, which is only possible if you will close one of his primary access points: your toxic emotions.

Exercises for Reflection and Discussion

1. What are the primary negative emotions you battle in your life? Examples include bitterness, jealousy, fear, and rage.

_____

_____

_____

_____

_____

_____

2. Make a list of the main people you have chronic negative feeling toward.

_____

_____

_____

_____

_____

_____

3. What thoughts do you have about God, others, or yourself that have been transmitted through negative emotions? Ask the Holy Spirit to help you with this question if something doesn't come to your mind. It may take you more than one day to answer this question.

_____

_____

_____

_____

_____

_____

4. Is there a relationship in your life that has been negatively affected or experienced division because of the accusations of the devil? Explain.

_____

_____

_____

_____

_____

_____

Applying Healing Principles

Complete the following steps to apply what you have learned in the lesson:

1. **Make a list of those you are or have been angry with and ask the Holy Spirit to help you realize any accusations the devil has made toward them.** This exercise is particularly important if your list includes your spouse or those close to you. Think about relationships that started well and then over time your thoughts and feelings became negative toward them. Were there hurts or unresolved anger that allowed the devil to slander them toward you?

2. **Make a commitment to deal with toxic emotions daily so as not to give the devil a foothold any longer.** Later in this book, I will address how to deal with toxic emotions daily.

3. **Begin a process of scrutinizing your thoughts more carefully, and don't assume all your thoughts originate within your own mind.** The Bible supplies the most important standard by which to measure your thoughts. If you recognize a thought is unbiblical, then you know it didn't originate with God, nor should it be allowed to influence you. You should reject it.

Healing Confession

Confess the following aloud:
I confess, in agreement with God's Word, that my negative emotions are an open door for the devil when I don't deal with them properly. I know I have authority over the devil because I am a child of God and don't need to fear him, but I do need to respect what he can do when I leave a door open to him. Because of that danger, I will vigilantly guard the door of my emotions. I will rid my life of any negative emotions I have carried from my past and any messages that the devil implanted in them. From this day forward, every day, I will deal with any toxic emotions I have so I can keep my heart healed, healthy, and safe from the enemy's attacks.

Healing Prayer

Silently or aloud, pray this prayer:

Father in Heaven, forgive me for any negative emotions I have harbored within my heart and have kept away from You. I repent of thoughts and feelings I held on to that have caused division in my relationships with others. Not only do I repent, but I also submit to You and will do whatever is necessary to make those relationships right.

Holy Spirit, You are the Spirit of Truth, and You know the depths of my heart and everything within me. I ask You to bring out every feeling and thought within me that is wrong and needs to be addressed. In the process, I ask You to heal my heart and every relationship in my life that the devil has damaged. Help me to break old habits and learn new habits and ways to deal with my emotions quickly and properly.

Devil, I take authority over you in Jesus' name. I take authority over every thought and feeling you have incited within me. I establish God's Word as the standard for my life and my thought life. I reject every thought that doesn't align with the standard of God's Word. I cast you out of my mind and emotions. In Jesus' name, amen.

Day 7

The Enemy of Our Emotions

When one of the scribes asked Jesus to name what is the greatest commandment, here is His reply:

Jesus answered him, *"The first of all the commandments is: 'Hear, O Israel, the Lord our God, the Lord is one. And you shall love the Lord your God with all your heart, with all your soul, with all your mind, and with all your strength.' This is the first commandment. And the second, like it, is this: 'You shall love your neighbor as yourself.' There is no other commandment greater than these."* (Mark 12:29–31)

Jesus was quoting from two important Old Testament passages, Deuteronomy chapter 6 and Leviticus chapter 19, but I want to focus on the first one. Jesus reaffirms that our love for God should come from *four major components* that make up our being: (1) our *hearts* are our spirits where God lives; (2) our *mind*s are our intellects; (3) our *bodies* are our physical existence and strength; and (4) He also included our *souls*. Jesus said, "Love the Lord your God [...] with all your soul." But what is your soul? It includes *your emotions and will*, which operate together. However, it is critical for us to understand how they work.

I have been discussing how the devil has access to our negative emotions when we don't deal with them properly. If we manage them in the right way, then he doesn't have access to them. The choice is ours. The mind, body, and spirit are easy to understand, but how do our souls operate? It depends on the person. Healthy people allow their wills to take charge of their emotions. Remember, the devil has access to our negative emotions when we manage them poorly. Paul wrote to Timothy, *"God has not given us a spirit of fear, but of love, and of power, and of a sound mind"* (2 Timothy 1:7). Did you know the devil will try to put fear on you so that you'll make a wrong decision? God will never honor a fear-based decision. He only rewards faith-based decisions. Our wills always have the ability to make the right decisions because they are the part of us that *should* be in control.

However, some people allow their emotions to take precedence over their will. The devil has access to our negative emotions, which may be very real, but that doesn't make them right. For example, I may be angry at someone and want to berate or even physically assault that person, but it doesn't mean it's right. Or I might be feeling fear concerning someone or something, and I act based on that fear. My response is the opposite of what God wants me to do. The fear may be very real, but that doesn't mean it's right.

If I want to experience inner healing, and remain healed and healthy, then I have a decision to make.

**I have to choose not to let my emotions
dictate my behavior.**

I won't let my emotions decide the way that I act and treat other people. With this shift in thought, my will now rules over my emotions. Even though the devil has access to my emotions, I don't have to deny my emotions—I can still let myself feel—but when there is a time that I shouldn't do something, my will has to take precedence over my emotions.

I may know I shouldn't do something, but I still really want to do it. My negative emotions will urge me to do the wrong thing anyway. Rather than my emotions controlling my life, I put my will in control. On the other hand, I may know that I should do something, but I don't want to do it. I know I *should* be nice and polite, or even forgive someone, but I really don't want to do any of those things. In that moment, my will has to override my emotions, so I can do the right thing regardless of my initial desires.

Courage and fear are not opposites. In fact, courage is not even the absence of fear. It is the *mastery* of fear. Do you know that heroes almost always feel fear? When you hear of individuals who have acted with great courage, don't think they weren't fearful—they just overrode it. Heroes are heroes because they have learned to act by their will rather than letting their emotions dictate their actions.

For the rest of your life, you're going to face situations and circumstances in which your will simply has to stand tall and take authority over your emotions. I can tell you from my own observations that the most painful lives I have ever seen in this world are those that are emotion-controlled. The most blessed lives are those where a person follows the will of God through the power of the Holy Spirit, and they do the right thing, regardless of the way they feel. Those people don't hurt others, and they don't allow other people to damage them in the process.

Yes, you have a soul, and it contains emotions, good or bad, right or wrong. However, you also have a will. And your will must take priority over your emotions. Don't give the devil a place in your soul.

HEALING FROM GOD'S WORD

But I say to you who hear: Love your enemies, do good to those who hate you, bless those who curse you, and pray for those who spitefully use you. To him who strikes you on the one cheek, offer the other also. And from him who takes away your cloak, do not withhold your tunic either. Give to everyone who asks of you. And from him who takes away your goods do not ask them back. And just as you want men to do to you, you also do to them likewise.

But if you love those who love you, what credit is that

to you? For even sinners love those who love them. And if you do good to those who do good to you, what credit is that to you? For even sinners do the same. And if you lend to those from whom you hope to receive back, what credit is that to you? For even sinners lend to sinners to receive as much back. But love your enemies, do good, and lend, hoping for nothing in return; and your reward will be great, and you will be sons of the Most High. For He is kind to the unthankful and evil. Therefore be merciful, just as your Father also is merciful.

Judge not, and you shall not be judged. Condemn not, and you shall not be condemned. Forgive, and you will be forgiven. Give, and it will be given to you: good measure, pressed down, shaken together, and running over will be put into your bosom. For with the same measure that you use, it will be measured back to you. (Luke 6:27–38)

Be sober, be vigilant; because your adversary the devil walks about like a roaring lion, seeking whom he may devour. Resist him, steadfast in the faith, knowing that the same sufferings are experienced by your brotherhood in the world. (1 Peter 5:8–9)

Jesus answered him, "The first of all the commandments is: 'Hear, O Israel, the Lord our God, the Lord is one. And you shall love the Lord your God with all your heart, with all your soul, with all your mind, and with all your strength.' This is the first commandment." (Mark 12:29–30)

HEALING TRUTHS

- When Jesus speaks about the first commandment, He is extremely specific that we are to love God with all our hearts, souls, minds, and strength. Every part of you exists for the purpose of knowing and loving God.

- Your emotions are an important gauge in your life. They tell you when things seem good or bad, happy or sad, and peaceful or troubled. But you must keep your emotions in check.

- The Lord enabled you with a will to keep your emotions in check. Your will can make good decisions despite some bad emotions. In fact, to be emotionally healed and healthy, you must subject your emotions to your will. The reason this is true is quite simple; your emotions may be real, but that doesn't mean they are *right*.

- The more you give in to negative emotions and act upon them, the worse your life will become. Giving in to your emotions leaves the doors and windows of your heart and mind open to the devil. Giving him free access to influence you.

- If you want to live in freedom and victory, then there is a simple, yet profound choice you will have to make. You must choose to make your decisions based on what is right according to God's Word, rather than allowing your emotions to control you.

- Almost all heroes experience fear. Courage isn't the absence of fear; it is the mastery of it. When you see a person of strong character living a successful life, you can know that almost all of them experience the same negative emotions you do. They have simply learned not to be controlled by them.

Exercises for Reflection and Discussion

1. What negative emotions do you struggle with the most?

_____

_____

_____

_____

_____

2. What negative consequences have you experienced because you acted upon negative emotions?

_____

_____

_____

_____

_____

3. How has acting upon negative emotions affected your relationships with God and other people?

_____

_____

_____

_____

_____

4. When was a specific time you wanted to act upon a negative emotion but didn't? What happened as a result?

_____

_____

_____

_____

_____

_____

Applying Healing Principles

Complete the following steps to apply what you have learned in the lesson:

1. **From this day forward, consciously choose to place your will above your emotions in the decisions you make.** There is nothing wrong with having feelings, but feelings can be inconsistent with reality, even when they are quite intense. Even more dangerous, the devil has access to your fallen feelings. If you subject your emotions to your will, then you shut the door on him.

2. **Begin to scrutinize your negative emotions.** If you are angry at someone, then examine your thoughts. Even if those thoughts seem to have originated within you, under-

stand that the devil may have introduced them to slander the other person and cause division in your relationship. Especially watch those thoughts in a marriage or other close relationships.

3. **As you begin to make faith-based choices that override your negative feelings, notice how your emotions turn positive.** If you are emotionally and spiritually healthy, then your will is like the train engine that drives everything, and your emotions become the caboose. As you make right decisions, right emotions follow. If, however, you are not healthy, then your emotions become the engine while your will becomes the caboose. Sadly, when your will is the caboose, you put God in last place and make an idol of your feelings. Even though He loves you, He won't bless you when you worship and serve your feelings instead of Him.

Healing Confession

Confess the following aloud:

I confess, in agreement with God's Word, that the most important commandment in my life is to love God with all my heart, soul, mind, and strength. I will love Him with all my soul and not allow the devil to corrupt me. I choose to put my will above my emotions. When my emotions are positive, I will praise the Lord and thank Him for that blessing. But when my emotions are negative, I will not allow them to cause me to sin, nor will I make poor decisions. I will quickly bring my emotions before the Lord as I deal with them obediently. From this day on, I choose to place my will over my emotions, and I will strive to obey God's Word, regardless of the way I feel.

Healing Prayer

Silently or aloud, pray this prayer:
Father in Heaven, I repent for all the times I have allowed negative feelings to control me. I confess that I have sometimes allowed my emotions to be more important than You and others around me. Because of what I have done, I gave the devil an opportunity to work in my life. I submit my emotions to You and ask You to give me the wisdom and empower me to act above them when they are wrong. Give me the power to change unhealthy habits in my life. I ask you to restore what the devil has robbed from me. As I turn my life and soul over to You, I ask that You will heal me, lead me, and bless me. I pray You will pour out Your Holy Spirit upon me and give me the strength to do what You desire. In Jesus' name, amen.

Day 8

The Hurt Whisperer

I want to go a little further in our conversation about how the devil tries to influence our negative emotions by introducing to you the concept of the *hurt whisperer*. What I'm referring to is the way the enemy attempts to interact with our hurts. We've already discussed how the devil tries to work with our negative emotions when we don't deal with them properly. When we experience anger, fear, jealousy, or any negative emotions, we open the door for the devil to work—unless we close it by processing those feelings correctly. The same type of damage happens when someone hurts us, and we don't sort out our feelings the right way. Some of those hurts may have happened years ago, and even after all this time, we still have a door left wide open for the devil to manipulate our emotions.

(Important note: The devil is not omnipresent. He can only be at one place at a time. But he has a host of demonic forces that do his work for him. When I refer to the devil and his work in our lives, I'm really talking about demonic forces under the devil's authority. We shouldn't fear these demons, because as believers we have authority over them. But we must understand that they are real and how they work. See Luke 10:19-20; Ephesians 6:10-20.)

The devil enters our minds through hurt from a person, a sin, a failure, or anything else that leaves a spiritual wound. He is more dangerous because he's cunning and stealthy. If the devil showed up with a red suit, pitchfork, and pointy tail, then it would be easy for us to see the things he's trying to do to us. However, that's not how he operates. In the Garden of Eden, Satan came to Adam and Eve in the form of a wily, stealthy serpent. The devil is also stealthy in our lives. He doesn't want us to know he's around.

The devil wants to secretly implant messages in our minds that will damage us. He does this through hurt.

In the Garden of Eden, the devil tempted Adam and Eve, and they sinned and fell. It was a devastating wound for them and all of humanity. After Adam and Eve sinned, God confronted them:

> *Then the Lord God called to Adam and said to him, "Where are you?"*
> *So he said, "I heard Your voice in the garden, and I was afraid because I was naked; and I hid myself."*
> *And He said, "Who told you that you were naked?*

Have you eaten from the tree of which I commanded you
that you should not eat?" (Genesis 3:9–11)

The devil tempted Adam and Eve, and they gave in and
sinned. *But the devil works both sides of sin's door. First, he*
tempts us, and then when we fail, he accuses us.

Remember Genesis tells us that God made Adam and Eve
naked, yet they had no shame at all (see Genesis 2:25). But
then the devil tempted them, and they sinned. Their disobe-
dience to God caused them to feel shame, so they hid from
God and covered themselves with fig leaves. Adam told God
he was hiding because he was naked. God asked, "Who told
you that you were naked?" But God doesn't ask questions
to get answers; He already knows the answer to everything.
What God was really saying was, "Adam, I didn't say that to
you. That thought didn't even originate within you. Someone
told you there was something wrong with your nakedness." As
soon as Adam and Eve sinned and experienced the pain of
their failure, they fell from God's grace. Immediately, the devil
swooped in and whispered to their souls, "You're defective.
There's something wrong with you. Your bodies are shameful,
and so is your nakedness." On top of their fallen state, they
had an implanted hurt, so they hid from God and each other.

We must realize that just as God has a will for our lives, so
does the devil. The devil's will is to keep us from a healthy relationship with a loving heavenly Father. The devil also doesn't
want us to experience healthy relationships with other people.

Thus, the minute he sees our pain, the devil starts whispering lies. The worst thing about our hurts is not the pain itself; it's the message in the pain. There's always a message.

As an adult survivor of childhood abuse, when you allow your mind to think back over your life, you remember the rejection and abuse. The devil, because he is so evil, tries to make children who have been abused think there's something wrong with them. Even in the moment of experiencing the abuse, the devil slithered up to you and whispered, "There's something wrong with you. You're the reason this awful thing is happening to you. God doesn't love you as much as He loves other people. You're a failure. You'll never succeed. You're cursed. Everything good you ever get, you'll lose. You're a burden. You're ugly." These messages get implanted inside us, and it's not just the pain of the rejection, abuse, or failure that causes the most harm; it's these lying messages the devil whispers to us in our pain.

I know how the devil works from the experiences in mine and Karen's past that gave the devil an opportunity to speak to us. I can honestly say I believed many of his messages. There had to be something wrong with me. For example, I was taller than my second-grade teacher—and six feet tall at the age of twelve. At one point, I was significantly taller than anyone else I knew who was my same age. Rather than feeling good about my height, I was sure there was something wrong with me. I always felt self-conscious about my appearance, but especially about my height. I thought of myself as "freakishly tall" and concluded I was, therefore, a freak. I believed the message that I was an oddity. But I need to tell you, I'm not a freak. I am *"fearfully and wonderfully made"* (Psalm 139:14), and so are you.

As you read this lesson, I want to encourage you to examine the pain of your past. How has the devil tried to whisper to you in that pain? He's been pulling the same trick since the days of Adam and Eve. Who told you God didn't love you? Who told you there was something wrong with you? Who told you that you're a failure? It was definitely *not God.* God's your friend and not your accuser. He is on your side. Did you produce these thoughts on your own? Let me tell you, I know you didn't. It was the *diabolos* who said these things to you. The devil is the hurt whisperer, and he's evil. He wants to take your fallen emotions, your hurts, and your pain and use them to slip through an open door and whisper lies to you. However, you are going to experience healing in your life today because you are going to uncover those lies and replace them with the truth of God's Word.

HEALING FROM GOD'S WORD

For I know the thoughts that I think toward you, says the Lord, thoughts of peace and not of evil, to give you a future and a hope. (Jeremiah 29:11)

There is therefore now no condemnation to those who are in Christ Jesus, who do not walk according to the flesh, but according to the Spirit. (Romans 8:1)

For He made Him who knew no sin to be sin for us, that we might become the righteousness of God in Him. (2 Corinthians 5:21)

Yet in all these things we are more than conquerors through Him who loved us. For I am persuaded that neither death nor life, nor angels nor principalities nor powers, nor things present nor things to come, nor height nor depth, nor any other created thing, shall be able to separate us from the love of God which is in Christ Jesus our Lord. (Romans 8:37–39)

HEALING TRUTHS

- The devil is so dangerous because he is cunning and stealthy. Since he first deceived Adam and Eve in the Garden of Eden, he has chosen trickery to mask his evil intentions.

- As soon as Adam and Eve sinned, they opened a door for the devil to whisper into their minds, "You are defective. You are naked, and it is wrong. You should be ashamed of yourselves." He told them these things, and they didn't even realize the devil was the one speaking to them.

- The devil's words to Adam and Eve were the opposite of God's will. They didn't understand it because they were unaware of his stealth and cunning. They didn't fully understand what had happened to them or who had done it.

- The truth is that the devil, by his demonic spirits, shows up at every sin, failure, tragedy, or loss. Then he tries to whisper his lies into your soul. He is the hurt whisperer whose full-time job is to take advantage of you when you're vulnerable. He whispers his deceptions at your most difficult moments so he can deceive you and defeat you.

- The devil uses sin, trauma, grief, and pain to create opportunities to deceive you. He can even use times of pride, popularity, or success to implant deceptive messages. There is one thing all His messages have in common: they disagree with and oppose God's Word. Then they threaten to derail God's plan for your life.

- If you want to experience emotional healing and health, then you must erase the demonic messages the devil implanted within you during both good times and bad.

Replace them with God's Word. Then ask the Holy Spirit
to help you uncover anywhere the hurt whisperer stealth-
ily implanted his lies and replace them with the truth of
God's Word.

Exercises for Reflection and Discussion

1. List the most traumatic events in your life.

_____

_____

_____

_____

_____

_____

**2. Did any of those events change you for the worse or
damage your relationship with God or others? Explain.**

_____

_____

_____

_____

_____

_____

3. What were the negative messages you received in any of those events, particularly messages against God, others, or yourself? Be as specific as possible.

_____

_____

_____

_____

_____

_____

4. List the messages you received because of positive events in your life when you were feeling successful, attractive, wealthy, powerful, or popular. Think about the best times in your life and consider if you received messages that were inconsistent with God's Word. Did they make you believe you did not need God? What were they?

_____

_____

_____

_____

_____

_____

Applying Healing Principles

Complete the following steps to apply what you have learned
in the lesson:

1. **Ask the Holy Spirit to help you uncover and erase every
    negative message the devil whispered into your mind in
    your past.** This process can take a few weeks, or several
    months. Some things will come to your mind immediately,
    but others may take time. The Holy Spirit knows your heart,
    and His timing is perfect.

2. **Every time you uncover a negative message, find a Scrip-
    ture to counter it.** The only thing powerful enough to over-
    come the devil's lies is God's Word.

3. **Confess those Scriptures every time the enemy tries to
    bring you back under their influence.** He will battle you
    and try to keep you in bondage, but the power of God's
    Word is all you need to defeat him. Don't trust your feelings
    because the devil will try to manipulate you with fear and
    guilt. Trust in God's love and the authority of His Word. He
    will set you free to live free forever. Begin confessing the

Scriptures now over every lie from your past that you uncover.

4. **Every time the devil tries to condemn you or put shame on you, begin to praise God for the blood of Jesus and the grace of God.** The devil hates to hear about the blood of Jesus and God's grace because they are what defeated him and set us free.

Healing Confession

Confess the following aloud:

I confess, in agreement with God's Word, that the devil is evil and stealthy. Since he first encountered Adam and Eve in the Garden of Eden, he has been using the same tactics to bring people into bondage, and he has done the same with me. I now uncover the devil's schemes in my life and take authority over him in Jesus' name. I also take authority over every lie he has spoken into my mind and spirit, in both good times and bad. I declare that I am more than a conqueror in Jesus and that, by God's grace, I am the righteousness of God in Christ. I declare that because of my faith in Jesus, I will never be condemned by God because His plan for my life is to give me peace, a future, and a hope. And I declare that God has welcomed me into His family, and my future will be full of life and love.

Healing Prayer

Silently or aloud, pray this prayer:

Holy Spirit, You have been with me at every moment of my life since the time of my conception. You know everything that has happened to me and how it has affected me. I now ask You to help me recognize every single lie the devil has whispered into my mind and heart since the day of my birth. In the good times and the tough times, whether I was aware or not, the devil lied to me. I ask you to reveal the lies he has told me. Holy Spirit, you are the Spirit of Truth. I now open my heart to You and pray You will help me replace the lies of the devil with the truth of God's Word. I need you to heal my mind and emotions from the damage that has been done in me through the devil's work. I also pray that You will forgive me for the things that I have done that have offended You or harmed others because of these lies. My desire, from this day forward, is to live to glorify God and fulfill His purpose for me. Give me the power to change and to do God's will. In Jesus' name, amen.

FINAL THOUGHTS ON SECTION THREE

Letting God Fight for Us

Life will inevitably send people along who will hurt you and who will say and do things to upset you. At times, you will get angry, or experience hurt. There's nothing wrong with those emotions; they are normal. As a human being, you will have negative emotions and hurt feelings. Many times, people will not say they are sorry for the harm they caused you. Some people may never take responsibility for their behavior. Even so, you must understand that when we harbor long-term anger, nurse bitterness, shelter unforgiveness, or hold onto too many other negative emotions about others, we damage ourselves. If you hold on to those feelings, then you do injury to yourself far worse than anyone else could do. If you are holding long-term anger toward someone, then you probably believe things about that person that are not true.

I want you to examine yourself carefully. Consider again the things you have learned in this section, meditate on the Scriptures, and confess to the Lord the truth about what you have in your heart. Allow the Holy Spirit to continue His work in your life in the areas where you are holding long-term negative emotions. Start by addressing any ongoing anger you hold, then choose today to forgive. From this day forward, you must understand that the devil has access to our negative emotions when we don't process them correctly. He uses them to enter our hearts and minds and do damage. Close the door to *diabolos*. Do not allow him back in. Only then can the Holy Spirit heal what's happened in your heart.

Your will is like a muscle, and the more you make right decisions, regardless of the way you feel, the stronger that muscle will become. You will reach a place where you make responsible decisions. Some people go through their entire lives identifying as victims, and they think to themselves, *I can't help it. I'm just devastated. I must act this way. People have hurt me.* I understand why they feel this way, so I'm not making fun of that response, but that's not a healthy way to live. You're going to continue experiencing hurt and hurting other people unless something changes.

If you want to live responsibly, then respond this way:

Lord, I'm going to love you with all my soul, my will, and my emotions. When I feel like it, I'm going to love you. But when I don't feel like it, I'm also going to love you. When I feel like loving other people, I'm going to love them. And when I don't, my will is going to override my emotions, and I'm going to do the right thing as You give me the strength, Lord. I am committed to living as a person in control of my will and my emotions.

The devil is the hurt whisperer, and he wants to gain access to your hurts. But I want you to let the Lord do the work He's wanting to do in your heart. For Him to take control, you will have to allow Him to uncover the messages that are embedded within the pain and failures of your life. As you go forward in life, recognize that every time something bad happens, the devil will try to whisper to you. He's the devil, and he's evil. I want you to understand that he's there, but he is not more powerful than God. The devil cannot do anything to you that you don't allow him to do because you have more access to power than he has.

Under the Lord, you have more authority than the devil does. The way he will try to hurt you is to get you to hurt yourself by accepting thoughts that are not from God. The thoughts the devil puts in your mind are designed to steal, kill, and destroy. Thus, every time something bad happens to you, or you experience hurt or pain, be aware. Don't let him whisper into your heart something that will hurt you or cause you to hurt yourself. Only listen to what the Word of God says. Take those thoughts captive (see Corinthians 10:5). Reject the hurt whisperer and replace his lies with the truth of God's Word. That is how healing will flow into your heart.

SECTION FOUR

GOD'S WORD AND OUR THOUGHTS

I want you to know how important the truth of the Word of God is in our lives. The more your thoughts line up with the truth of God's Word, the healthier you will become.

Day 9

The Word of Truth

God can only operate in an environment of truth, and the devil only works in an environment of deception and lies. Thus, when you are walking in truth, you're walking with God and allowing Him to work within your life, but first, you must decide what your relationship with the truth will be.

Jesus prays for His followers and requests that His Father would *"sanctify them by Your truth. Your word is truth"* (John 17:17). Paul writes to Timothy, *"All scripture is given by inspiration of God, and is profitable for doctrine, for reproof, for correction, for instruction in righteousness, that the man of God may be complete, thoroughly equipped for every good work"* (2 Timothy 3:16). The Greek word translated here as *"inspiration"* actually means *"God-breathed."* Paul is saying Scripture is the breath of God—it is *alive.*

When you allow the Word into your life, you are allowing God in.

And if you allow the Word in, then it's going to heal you. The psalmist writes, *"God sent His word to heal them and to deliver them from all of their destruction"* (Psalm 107:20, my paraphrase). God has given us phenomenal hardware—our brains. He created them but, left to fend for ourselves, we have some serious software problems. The Word of God is the software on which our hardware was designed to run. Every time you accept the truth, and every time you read the Bible, the Bible reads you and reprograms you because it is alive.

The writer of Hebrews says, *"For the word of God is living and powerful, and sharper than any two-edged sword, piercing even to the division of soul and spirit, and of joints and marrow, and is a discerner of the thoughts and intents of the heart"* (Hebrews 4:12). When God's Word gets inside of you, it's like a living two-edged sword at work. One edge operates as a surgeon's scalpel to heal us and to remove that which doesn't belong. The other edge operates as a sword which seeks out the enemies inside of us and destroys them. No wonder the devil hates the Word of God. Remember, the first thing that the devil ever said to a human being was *"Has God indeed said...?"* (Genesis 3:1). The devil tried to sow doubt about God's Word from the very beginning. The devil knows the Word of God is the sword of the Spirit. Paul described the power of God's Word to the Ephesians, and in a sense, he told them that it is *nuclear* (see Ephesians chapter 6)! It is a powerful weapon. Therefore, when you get the Word of God inside of you, it reprograms you from the inside out and wins the battle for you.

The psalmist wrote that a person who constantly meditates on God's Word will succeed in everything he or she does (see Psalm 1:1-3). Why is this true? Because if you're reading and meditating on the Bible, then you're downloading the right software for nurturing your marriage, raising your children, managing your finances, or navigating your relationships. You are especially accessing the correct data for how to interact with God. When the Word of God gets inside of you, it reprograms you for success in every single area of your life. I strongly encourage you right now to make the choice that God's Word will take its rightful place in your life.

Are you merely dating God's Word, or have you married it? In other words, do you have a "convenient" relationship with the Bible? Do you only look at it when you're in a crisis? When the Bible says something with which you don't agree, what do you do? For example, if your friend advises you to do something you know goes against the Bible, do you follow the Word, or do you take your friend's counsel? If you go to see an "expert" who encourages you to do something that is against the Bible, do you believe the expert or the Bible?

The Bible is not a legalistic book of do's and don'ts. No, it's a book of love. But God designed you and every area of your life to operate according to His Word. It is the master instruction manual for humanity. If you want to know how to think, talk, act, or how to embrace the right ethical or moral point of view, then you will find all those answers in the Bible.

I want you to understand that your relationship with

the Word of God is going to determine how healed you will become. I've told you about the devil, the hurt whisperer. I have discussed the things people say and do that hurt you. You must replace those hurts and lies with the Word. When God comes in to heal you and do His work, He will do it by His Word. When you have wrong thoughts about other people, they all must be replaced with the Word.

When Karen and I got married, she was devastated emotionally. She thought of herself as ugly. She even believed God didn't love her. At one point, she began to think she was actually insane and had some serious mental disorder. However, every day, Karen woke up and read the Bible. It was her daily habit. Even though she read the Bible every day, she didn't believe the parts of the Scripture that told her God loved her, but she read it anyway. I witnessed what happened next. Over days, weeks, months, and years, God started transforming my wife. Today, Karen is one of the most emotionally healthy people on earth. And she still reads the Bible every day. She meditates on it and processes it. She has replaced the devil's lies with the truth of God's Word. In the process, the wounds of her life were healed, and she has become the person God created her to be rather than staying the person the devil convinced her she was.

Yes, I want you to marry the Bible right now. I want you to believe that it's God's Word for you. If you do, then I know it is going to come in and heal you and make you into a strong person of faith who can live a functional, healthy life, and relate to people the way that you should. The Bible is the Word of God, and it must be the standard for your life.

HEALING FROM GOD'S WORD

All Scripture is given by inspiration of God, and is profitable for doctrine, for reproof, for correction, for instruction in righteousness, that the man of God may be complete, thoroughly equipped for every good work. (2 Timothy 3:16–17)

For the word of God is living and powerful, and sharper than any two-edged sword, piercing even to the division of soul and spirit, and of joints and marrow, and is a discerner of the thoughts and intents of the heart. (Hebrews 4:12)

Blessed is the man
Who walks not in the counsel of the ungodly,
Nor stands in the path of sinners,
Nor sits in the seat of the scornful;
But his delight is in the law of the Lord,
And in His law he meditates day and night.
He shall be like a tree
Planted by the rivers of water,
That brings forth its fruit in its season,

Whose leaf also shall not wither;
And whatever he does shall prosper. (Psalm 1:1–3)

Therefore whoever hears these sayings of Mine, and does them, I will liken him to a wise man who built his house on the rock: and the rain descended, the floods came, and the winds blew and beat on that house; and it did not fall, for it was founded on the rock.

But everyone who hears these sayings of Mine, and does not do them, will be like a foolish man who built his house on the sand: and the rain descended, the floods came, and the winds blew and beat on that house; and it fell. And great was its fall. (Matthew 7:24–27)

HEALING TRUTHS

- God will only do His work in an atmosphere of truth. Conversely, the devil will only do his work in an atmosphere of deception. Obviously, we all want God to work in our lives rather than the devil, so we must make the choice to walk in truth and not in deception.

- Jesus defined what truth is—God's Word. We must understand that the Bible is not on par with any other book. It is the most important book ever written because it is *the standard* of truth for all areas of our lives. For healing and health to be a reality in your life, you must first establish God's Word as the standard of truth by which you will live.

- Victorious people share a common trait: they have "married" the Word of God and chosen to live by it. These aren't perfect people by any means, but they are simply devout in their commitment to the Bible as God's inerrant and inspired Word. It is the truth without any mixture of error at all for them. They stay unwavering in the face of criticism and opposition because they have experienced the power of God working in their lives when they believed and obeyed His Word.

- Chronically defeated believers also share a common thread: they have a convenient relationship with the Bible. They are "dating" it, yet they haven't committed to a life-long relationship. They treat Scripture as they would a cafeteria line, where they take what they want and leave what they don't want. They like to skip over the most nutritious parts and only eat dessert. As a result, they are spiritually weak and anemic.

- Obeying God's Word is an act of love and worship to Jesus, and it allows the Holy Spirit to work in your life. God always loves you unconditionally, but your faith in His Word is what allows Him to do His most powerful work in your life, and it releases His incredible blessings to you.

- If you want to be healed, healthy, and mature, then you must get to the point where you draw a firm line in the sand and say, "Today, I choose to marry God's Word, and from this day forth, it will be *the* standard of truth for my life. When my emotions, passions, or thoughts disagree with God's Word, I will then choose God's truth and obey it. When my friends, family, the experts, or the crowd disagree with the Bible, I still choose His Word and obey it." When you make this simple choice, you open the door for the Spirit of Truth to heal you and set you free. At the same time, you shut the door on the devil, the deceiver, and end his reign of terror in your life.

Exercises for Reflection and Discussion

1. If you were to be honest, how would you describe your relationship with God's Word up to this point in your life?

_____

_____

_____

_____

_____

_____

2. As you commit to obeying God's Word, what fears do you have, and from where do you think they originate?

_____

_____

_____

_____

_____

3. What do you think will happen because of obeying God's Word? Do you think you might be labeled a "fanatic" or lose a friend as a result? Why or why not?

_____

_____

_____

_____

_____

4. When was a time in your life when you knowingly disobeyed God's Word? What were the results?

_____

_____

_____

_____

_____

_____

Applying Healing Principles

Complete the following steps to apply what you have learned in the lesson:

1. **Right now, decide the Bible will be _the_ standard for truth in your life.** Commit to obeying it above any other source. Do what the Bible says even when it is difficult or inconvenient. Stand up for God and His Word, even while you live in a rebellious culture.

2. **Set a time every day to read God's Word and pray.** You may have heard of a practice called a "quiet time" or a "daily devotional." Every day for over forty-eight years, Karen and I have risen each morning to read the Bible and pray separately or together, which I will describe in

more detail later in this book. It keeps us close to the Lord, spiritually healthy, emotionally healed, and healthy for each other. Personally, I begin by writing one or two pages in my journal. I record thoughts about what is currently going on in my life and in my relationship with the Lord. I write what the Lord is speaking to me. Then I use an online daily Bible, which includes readings from the Old Testament and New Testament. Through this plan, I can read the entire Bible every year. There are also printed Bibles that can help you accomplish the same goal. After I have journaled and read the Bible, I pray. I try to make sure my prayers are very relational and honest. I treat the Lord as my loving Dad who cares about every single issue in my life. This part of my day is the most important.

Healing Confession

Confess the following aloud:

I confess, in agreement with God's Word, that God's Word is the standard of all truth. It is the standard of truth in my life above anything or anyone else. From this day forward, I make a total commitment of my life to God's Word. I will read it, believe it, and, with the Holy Spirit's help, I will obey it and live by it. The Word of God will set the standard in my life of what is right and wrong. I will seek out the wisdom of God's Word for my life because, by it, I will succeed in everything I do.

Healing Prayer

Silently or aloud, pray this prayer:

Holy Spirit, You are the Spirit of Truth. I invite You into my life. You inspired every writer of the Bible. You understand the Scriptures better than anyone, so I ask You to give me insight and understanding as I read and meditate on God's Word. Lead me into mental and emotional health and replace error with Your truth. When I have thoughts that don't agree with Your Word, help me identify and replace them with the truth. I commit completely to Your truth and forsake deception, compromise, and dishonesty. I now open my heart to You because You know every thought and feeling within me. By Your love and grace, work in my life until only truth remains, and I am healed and set free. In Jesus' name, amen.

Day 10

The Battle for Our Thoughts

One of the most important things we do in life is to choose our thoughts. When I first got saved, I had all kinds of thoughts running through my mind. At the time, I didn't realize I could choose my thoughts because I shouldn't have had a lot of the ones I was having, and I really didn't know how to deal with them. Over time, however, God began to heal my thoughts. And part of the healing He is going to do in your life will happen as you learn to take your thoughts captive.

If you have heard of the concept of spiritual warfare, understand that it is real. I admit that when I first heard about it, I thought, *I don't want to be involved with that. Why would I want to fight the devil? The whole idea of spiritual warfare sounds weird to me.*

However, spiritual warfare isn't strange like I once thought. In fact, it's not unusual at all. What we do in spiritual warfare is quite practical because most of it occurs in our minds. The apostle Paul writes, *"Though we walk in the flesh, we do not war according to the flesh. For the weapons of our warfare are not carnal but mighty in God for pulling down strongholds, casting down arguments and every high thing that exalts itself against the knowledge of God, bringing every thought into captivity to the obedience of Christ"* (2 Corinthians 10:3–5). Paul says the weapons of our warfare are not carnal, meaning they don't come from our human flesh; they come from a divine source. What we do with those weapons is fight against the devil's arguments and everything that tries to exalt itself against the knowledge of God. That means the devil works full-time to create strongholds within our thoughts. These include strongholds of fear, jealousy, thoughts of low self-esteem, and a sense of rejection, among other things.

Our bondage is built on a foundation of thoughts. If you have an addiction, then it is constructed by the way you think—Zig Ziglar called it "stinkin' thinkin.'" How, then, do you deal with these kinds of thoughts? You take those thoughts captive because any thought you don't take captive will take *you* captive.

When the devil encountered Jesus after a 40-day fast in the wilderness, he tried to attack Jesus through his thoughts. Three times Satan told Jesus a half-truth or a lie. And, three times Jesus responded with the words, *"it is written"* (see Matthew 4:1–11). The greatest battle ever fought on the earth was between the devil's thoughts and Jesus' thoughts.

Jesus won because He relied on God's Word—His Word is always greater than the devil's lies.

But you must know, *your* thoughts are not greater than the devil's thoughts. If you're going to battle the devil with only what is in your head, then you're destined to lose. You need God's thoughts on any matter.

Paul told the Corinthian believers to take every thought captive to the obedience of Christ. The word translated "captive" means "to capture at the point of a spear." This is enemy warfare, and the enemy has taken ground in your mind. You must put a spear point to that thought and capture it. The word translated "obedience" in this passage means "to listen underneath." God's Word, and not your thoughts, should be the supreme authority in your life. You are not under the authority of anyone else's thoughts—certainly not the devil's. Any time a thought comes into my mind, I make it listen to what Jesus has to say. If my mind says, "You're no good, and God doesn't love you," then I can tell you I'm not going to go through life believing I'm no good and God doesn't love me. My thoughts might say, "You've done too much wrong, so you can't be forgiven. Everybody hates you. Nobody really likes you. You're always going to lose. You're always going to be rejected. You're never going to be able to keep anything good in your life. You're cursed." It is then that I pick up my spear, and under the power of the Holy Spirit, I go to battle.

I know when these thoughts come into my life because they don't agree with God's Word. I know that today, but I didn't always know or believe that. I had toxic thoughts trying to take up real estate within my mind. The devil was using them to hurt me, upset me, and cause me to act and believe false things. I had to learn to take my thoughts captive to the obedience of Christ. I am not saying you can take a thought out of your mind, but you can replace it with a greater thought. If I were to tell you not to think about something, then that is exactly what you will think about. What I am telling you is that the Word of God must replace those lying thoughts.

Yes, you will have hurts in your life, which could even happen today, and the devil's going to do his best to whisper thoughts into your mind. However, those thoughts turn into *strongholds* if you allow them to be exalted over the knowledge of God. The devil doesn't want you to know or relate to God. Consequently, he is going to try to tell you things about God, others, and yourself that are not true. That is when you must take your thoughts captive. The devil can't do that for you, and God won't do it for you; only you can take your thoughts captive. When something in your mind doesn't agree with God's Word, then it is time to act and act quickly. Reject those thoughts and replace them with the truth of the Bible. This action is the key to your healing, freedom, health, and success on every level. Today, I urge you to begin by examining your thoughts. Then begin the process of taking those thoughts captive to Christ and letting Him overcome them.

HEALING FROM GOD'S WORD

Then Jesus said to those Jews who believed Him, "If you abide in My word, you are My disciples indeed. And you shall know the truth, and the truth shall make you free." (John 8:31–32)

How can a young man cleanse his way?
By taking heed according to Your word.
With my whole heart I have sought You;
Oh, let me not wander from Your commandments!
Your word I have hidden in my heart,
That I might not sin against You.
Blessed are You, O Lord!
Teach me Your statutes.
With my lips I have declared
All the judgments of Your mouth.
I have rejoiced in the way of Your testimonies,
As much as in all riches.
I will meditate on Your precepts,
And contemplate Your ways.
I will delight myself in Your statutes;
I will not forget Your word. (Psalm 119:9–16)

Finally, my brethren, be strong in the Lord and in the power of His might. Put on the whole armor of God, that you may be able to stand against the wiles of the devil.

For we do not wrestle against flesh and blood, but against principalities, against powers, against the rulers of the darkness of this age, against spiritual hosts of wickedness in the heavenly places. Therefore take up the whole armor of God, that you may be able to withstand in the evil day, and having done all, to stand. Stand therefore, having girded your waist with truth, having put on the breastplate of righteousness, and having shod your feet with the preparation of the gospel of peace; above all, taking the shield of faith with which you will be able to quench all the fiery darts of the wicked one. And take the helmet of salvation, and the sword of the Spirit, which is the word of God; praying always with all prayer and supplication in the Spirit, being watchful to this end with all perseverance and supplication for all the saints. (Ephesians 6:10–18)

HEALING TRUTHS

- The psalmist writes that God sent His Word, first, to heal us, and second, to deliver us from our destructions, which means our sins and bondages (see Psalm 107:20). The writer of Hebrews reveals a supernatural truth about the Word of God: it is living and powerful and *"sharper than any two-edged sword"* (Hebrews 4:12). When the Word enters us, it is both alive and powerful. One edge of the sword serves as a scalpel that produces healing in places no one else can go, while the other is a sword fashioned to attack the enemy as he tries to destroy us.

- Paul says that we don't fight the devil with the flesh. He then tells us that the weapons we use to fight the devil are *"mighty in God for pulling down strongholds"* (2 Corinthians 10:4). Paul means that by God's power, we have everything we need to defeat the enemy.

- The enemy tries to establish mental strongholds to keep us from knowing and serving God. Paul says we are to use our spiritual weapons to "cast down arguments." These are the thoughts within us that oppose God and His Word.

- Paul also tells us to cast down "every high thing that exalts itself against the knowledge of God." He is referring to human pride, unbelief, cynicism, deception, the fear of other people, and lies the devil implants within our hearts when we go through pain or other difficulties. Any thoughts we have that oppose God's Word and His work must be cast down so we can be healed and set free.

- Paul concludes with a powerful statement, saying that we should bring "every thought into captivity to the obedience of Christ." This part of what he says is the most important. In our spiritual warfare against the devil, we must bring every thought "into captivity," which means to put a spear to the neck of our thoughts and command them to obey. Paul uses militant language because we are dealing with our mortal enemy.

- Any thought you don't take captive will take *you* captive. Rogue thoughts that don't align with God's Word are like enemy landmines that we must decisively root out. Spiritual warfare consists of us taking authority over thoughts in our minds and making them listen to what Jesus has to say. If our thoughts agree with Jesus, then we allow them to stay, but if they don't, then we are to treat them as though they are poison planted in us by the enemy, which then must be expelled and replaced with the truth.

Exercises for Reflection and Discussion

1. Are there thoughts in your mind right now that you know don't agree with God's Word? If so, what are they? For example, what do you believe about yourself? Or what do you believe God's Word says about you?

_____

_____

_____

_____

_____

_____

2. What happens in your life when you allow negative thoughts? How does it make you feel and act?

_____

_____

_____

_____

_____

_____

3. How have negative thoughts inhibited you or changed your ability to relate to God and trust Him?

_____

_____

_____

_____

_____

_____

Applying Healing Principles

Complete the following steps to apply what you have learned in the lesson:

1. **Understand that your mind is the primary battleground where the enemy seeks to hold you in bondage.** You must be vigilant about your thoughts to be healed and set free.

2. **Understand that the Word of God is *the* standard by which you examine your thoughts.** As you challenge your thoughts and force them to submit to Jesus and God's Word, you are doing direct and strategic spiritual warfare against the devil, and the weapons God has given to you are powerful enough to defeat him.

3. **Make a list of the negative thoughts in your mind that you know don't agree with God's Word.** Then find a Scripture to counter each of those thoughts. Openly renounce the lies in your mind and confess the Word of God as truth. As you do this, the two-edged sword of God's Word will defeat the enemy. You may have to do this many times before the enemy is completely defeated in your mind, but the process of confession and warfare makes you extraordinarily strong in the faith.

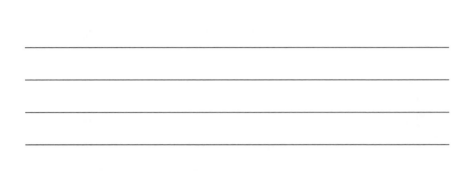

Healing Confession

Confess the following aloud:

I agree with God's Word and confess that every thought in my mind must surrender to the authority of Jesus. I will take every thought captive to the obedience of Christ. Only the thoughts that agree with God's Word will be allowed to influence my behavior. Every other thought will be examined and rejected. I will pursue God's Word in my life daily and allow it to do its full work as God's two-edged sword to heal my heart and defeat the devil.

Healing Prayer

Silently or aloud, pray this prayer:

Jesus, You are my Lord and Savior. I surrender every thought to You. Forgive me of the thoughts I have allowed in my life that argued against Your truth and prevented me from knowing and serving You as I should. I now surrender to You and agree that the thoughts I haven't taken captive have taken me captive. I thank You that You have given me the powerful weapon of Your Word to confront and defeat the devil and to tear down every stronghold and high place in my mind.

Holy Spirit, help me to replace every wrong thought in my mind with the truth of Your Word. In Jesus' name, amen.

FINAL THOUGHTS ON SECTION FOUR

Winning with the Word

As I've said, I received Christ over 48 years ago, but I can remember the time when I met Jesus, and He saved me. I honestly didn't know one verse in the Bible. Karen and I went to church for the first time and heard the preacher say, "Well, turn in your Bibles to ..." For one thing, I didn't even own a Bible, let alone have the foggiest idea of what he was talking about.

Honestly, when I first came to Jesus, my life had fallen apart—I was a mess. Everything I thought should work, didn't. I tried on my own to carry so many hurts and had multitudes of unresolved issues. But one thing was going right for me: I genuinely loved Jesus. Over the last five decades, the journey that Karen and I have taken is to learn what the Bible has to say and then apply it to our lives.

God will love you no matter what by His grace. You don't have to be a Bible scholar to get His attention or earn His love. He is madly in love with you right where you are. Nevertheless, the Bible will show you how to live and succeed. Don't think of it merely as a religious book because it's much more than that. It's a very practical book, and it's alive. When you make a habit of reading the Bible every day, you allow it to get inside of you. If you don't understand it right away, keep plowing through. Meditate on God's Word, and it will heal you. With it, you will be able to destroy all the works of the devil in your life. Commit to a daily relationship with the Word of God, and you'll see dramatic results in your life.

Jesus said that if we were His disciples, then we would abide in His Word, and we would know the truth, and the truth would make us free. Lies are what hold us in bondage. But how are you supposed to know if what you're thinking is true or not? Compare it to God's Word, that's how. Jesus said, *"Father, sanctify them in the truth. Your word is truth"* (John 17:17, my paraphrase). When something agrees with the Word of God, the Bible, then you can believe it's true, and it's going to set you free.

Bondage happens in our thoughts, so Paul tells us we must take our thoughts captive. That is what spiritual warfare is all about. It's the demanding work of examining every thought in your mind as it compares the truth of God's Word. If your thoughts agree with the Word, then they are the truth. If a thought is the truth, then nurture it and let it stay. You want those kinds of thoughts in your mind. However, if it opposes the truth, then reject it immediately because it came from the enemy. Don't let the devil build a stronghold in your mind because it will create a barrier between you and God and keep you in bondage.

When I got saved, I was in bondage in so many areas of my life, but I'm so thankful today. I'm not better than anyone else, but Jesus is. And I'm thankful that through studying the Bible, learning what it says, and allowing it to fill my mind, God has healed me and transformed my life. I promise, He will do the same for you.

SECTION FIVE

THE HEALING POWER OF FORGIVENESS

I call the issue I'm going to address in this section "the mother of all issues related to emotional healing." That is the issue of forgiveness. When we come to Jesus, all of us have people in our past who have hurt or disappointed us. You may be thinking of someone in your life right now who has hurt you or is actively hurting you now. Or you might be struggling with bitterness and unforgiveness. This section is critical to your inner healing.

Day 11

A Practice That Is Not Optional

I have already discussed how the devil accesses our negative emotions when we don't deal with them properly. He works with fear, jealousy, and anger. But one of the devil's favorite emotions to manipulate is unforgiveness because it gives him a foothold in our lives. The apostle Paul knew the dangers of bitterness and how it grieves the Holy Spirit, and that is why he wrote about it to the believers in Ephesus (see Ephesians 4:25–32). Unforgiveness is like an invisible umbilical cord that ties us to the pain of our past and keeps feeding our minds and hearts with toxic thoughts and emotions.

An offense against you might have happened ten years ago or yesterday. For some, it happened thirty years ago, and the offender is already dead. In every case, we need to deal with it so we can be healed.

About thirty-five years ago, I was a pastor of a church with a man who did some things and said some things to me that were devastating at that point in my life. I didn't know how to process my emotions toward him. All I knew was that I had grown to hate him. Eventually, I learned to forgive, but before that, unforgiveness had a damaging effect on me.

I hated him, and I couldn't see how I could ever forgive him. But holding onto those negative emotions changed me. First, it started to change the way I was treating my wife. She didn't do anything to deserve it, but I started venting my anger toward the man I hated on her. You see, it doesn't matter who caused your anger; the people who are closest to you will suffer the most in the fallout of your wrath. I was so angry at this man that I became short-tempered and my wife, Karen, was in the firing line, as were my children. You may have held anger toward someone for twenty years—it's still eating you up and affecting the way you relate to everyone else. Unforgiveness works that way; it starts to oppress us. I admit that I felt oppressed in both my thinking and my emotions, and finally, it affected my behavior. I was becoming increasingly bitter and cynical because unforgiveness was ruling my life.

I want to be as clear as possible:
forgiveness is not an option.

God commanded us to forgive. One day, Peter asked Jesus how many times we should forgive someone who offends us. Peter asked, "Lord, how many times do we forgive? Seven?" And Jesus said, "No seventy times seven." And then Jesus told Peter a parable about a servant who was forgiven a massive sum of money by his master—as much as ten million dollars. But incredibly, the same servant refused to forgive his fellow servant for an amount that was about a thousand dollars. The hypocrisy of the servant was clear to all of Jesus' listeners. Then Jesus closed the trap; He was teaching about how God forgives us, but how we often think we don't have to forgive other people (Matthew 18:21–35, my paraphrase).

Jesus was telling His followers that God has forgiven them more than they can even imagine. But He expects us to forgive others when they have offended us in return, even when they owe us a debt. Forgiveness is about writing off debts and returning the balance to zero, telling someone they no longer owe you anything. It is required whether the other person apologizes or not. It is saying, *"I'm forgiving you and turning the matter over to God. He may require more of you, but our account is settled."*

Many times, we want forgiveness from God, but we refuse to extend it to others. Jesus plainly says it doesn't work that way. In the parable He told, Jesus said the master sent the unforgiving servant to prison to be tormented until he repaid every cent of the original debt. Do you see the connection? Unforgiveness is a prison of torment. It gives the devil an opening to come into our lives and allows him to oppress us through bitterness, unforgiveness, unresolved anger, confusion, and depression. The devil slithers into our minds through the bitterness we are nursing and tells us more lies about those who have hurt us. He wants to keep us upset because it changes the way we relate to everyone. That's exactly what happened to me.

I want to lead you through a process of forgiveness in this lesson. I encourage you first to ask yourself who in your life you have not forgiven. Then, we will look at how to gain inner healing from the damage that's been done by both the offender and our own ongoing unforgiveness.

HEALING FROM GOD'S WORD

But I say to you who hear: Love your enemies, do good to those who hate you, bless those who curse you, and pray for those who spitefully use you. To him who strikes you on the one cheek, offer the other also. And from him who takes away your cloak, do not withhold your tunic either. (Luke 6:27–29)

Judge not, and you shall not be judged. Condemn not, and you shall not be condemned. Forgive, and you will be forgiven. (Luke 6:37)

Then Peter came to Him and said, "Lord, how often shall my brother sin against me, and I forgive him? Up to seven times?"

Jesus said to him, "I do not say to you, up to seven times, but up to seventy times seven. Therefore the kingdom of Heaven is like a certain king who wanted to settle accounts with his servants. And when he had begun to settle accounts, one was brought to him who owed him ten thousand talents. But as he was not able to pay, his master commanded that he be sold, with his wife and children and all that he had, and that payment be made. The servant therefore fell down before him, saying, 'Master, have patience with me, and I will pay you all.' Then the master of that servant was moved with compassion, released him, and forgave him the debt.

But that servant went out and found one of his fellow servants who owed him a hundred denarii; and he laid hands on him and took him by the throat, saying, 'Pay me what you owe!' So his fellow servant fell down at his feet and begged him, saying, 'Have patience with me, and I will pay you all.' And he would not, but went and threw him into prison till he should pay the debt. So when his fellow servants saw what had been done, they were very grieved, and came and told their master all that had been done. Then his master, after he had called him, said to him, 'You wicked servant! I forgave you all that debt because you begged me. Should you not also have had compassion on your fellow servant, just as I had pity on you?' And his master was angry, and delivered him to the torturers until he should pay all that was due to him.

So My heavenly Father also will do to you if each of you, from his heart, does not forgive his brother his trespasses." (Matthew 18:21–35)

HEALING TRUTHS

- It is impossible to be emotionally healed and healthy without forgiving those in our past or present that have hurt or offended us. Unforgiveness is like an invisible umbilical cord that connects us to the negative events and people of our lives. When we don't or won't forgive, we leave a door open for the devil to constantly feed bitterness, negativity, and bad memories to our minds and hearts.

- Even though we might be bitter or unforgiving toward someone in our past who we don't see anymore or who might have even died, those closest to us get the fallout of our negative emotions. It might be a parent, step-parent, ex-spouse, ex-friend, or ex-business partner who hurt or offended you in the past, but everyone else in proximity to you ends up paying the price.

- If we want to be healed and set free, then forgiveness isn't something we do only a few times in life to experience full healing and freedom. It must become a daily discipline in our lives. Every day, we deal with difficult and sometimes even abusive people, but going to bed with unresolved anger gives the devil a foothold in our lives to do his evil work. Dealing with toxic emotions must become a daily practice.

- Jesus taught us to pray every day for God to forgive us for our sins against Him, just as we forgive the sins of others. Notice that it is a conditional, simultaneous transaction. God doesn't give us the option of being forgiven when we don't forgive others. He gives us just as much grace as we are willing to give away to others. God forgoes judgment on us if we do so for others.

- In one of Jesus' final moments on the cross, He forgave those who betrayed and crucified Him. As His children, He requires us to walk according to His spirit and grace. If we follow His example, then we must forgive and release others to God, even those who have hurt or offended us. Only then will we be healed and set free.

Exercises for Reflection and Discussion

1. List those you have something against and have yet to forgive. Forgiving someone doesn't mean you have to like them or spend time with that person. It means you don't nurse feeling of resentment, nor will you talk negatively or wish terrible things on them.

_____

_____

_____

_____

_____

_____

2. Who are the people in your past or present who have done the worst things to you, hurt you, or offended you? Have you forgiven them? Explain.

_____

_____

_____

_____

_____

_____

3. How has unforgiveness affected those closest to you?

_____

_____

_____

_____

_____

_____

_____

4. What are the most difficult emotional problems you face? How are any of these connected to unforgiveness or bitterness? For example, you might list depression. Anger and unforgiveness are the highest emotional consumers in our lives. Since we only have a limited amount of emotional energy, when anger and unforgiveness have been active within us for an exceptionally long time, we can become emotionally exhausted and depressed. Or you might list anger and relational problems which can stem from unforgiveness.

_____

_____

_____

_____

_____

_____

Applying Healing Principles

Complete the following steps to apply what you have learned in the lesson:

1. **If you have harbored long-term anger or bitterness toward someone, then repent to God for the sin of unforgiveness.** Unforgiveness isn't merely a problem to be solved; it is a sin against God.

2. **Release your "right" to judge every person on your list and turn the matter over to God.** When you forgive, it means you're entrusting God with the person who offended you, trusting that His judgments are correct. Then, it is up to God to deal with that individual. Harboring unforgiveness is the same as telling God you don't trust Him, His intelligence, or His character when it comes to dealing with the person you have yet to forgive. Bitterness stems from a spirit that demands justice before you are willing to move on. Remember, however, if you want justice from someone else, it means you are also under that same justice. Don't hope someone gets "what they deserve"—because the same will happen to you. God gives grace for grace and justice for justice.

3. **Go through the list you made of the people you have yet to forgive and specifically, by name, release them to God and give them grace.** Speak every name on the list and

ask the Holy Spirit to help uncover any lies the devil has spoken to you about each person. Ask Him to help you see the people on your list through His eyes. In the previous lesson, I told you that the devil is an accuser and a slanderer. He gains a foothold into our lives through anger and negative emotions. Specifically, when we go to bed angry, he uses that as a doorway to accuse other people to us. I will say again: If you have gone to bed angry at someone, then you have been counseled by the devil, and you may not even know it. He is both stealthy and cunning. He will quickly use the doorway of unforgiveness to deceive us about others and cause disunity in our relationships. Consequently, when you have harbored unforgiveness for a long time, you have thoughts toward another person that are simply wrong. While you may be justifiably angry, the other person is still God's child, and He sees the good in them. If you want to be healed of unforgiveness, then you will have to learn to see people the way God sees them and not as enemies to be destroyed.

Healing Confession

Confess the following aloud:
Lord, I confess, in agreement with Your Word, that You have saved me by Your grace and forgiven all my sins. Because of the grace I have received from Jesus, I make a choice to give grace to others. I will walk in love and forgiveness. To those

who hurt or offend me, I will give grace and trust God to deal with them. From this day forward, I cut the umbilical cord connecting me to the hurts of my past, and I choose to walk forward in the grace of God.

Healing Prayer

Silently or aloud, pray this prayer.

Jesus, I know my sins and the sins of others put You on the cross and caused You such pain, but despite it, You have been so gracious to me. You saved me from the consequences of my sins and gave me eternal life. You have done all this freely, despite all the pain my sins caused You. I repent for harboring unforgiveness and pettiness toward others. I repent of hypocrisy, where on the one hand I want grace from you, but then, on the other, I want to judge others harshly. Today, I sincerely change my heart and mind about my sins and pray for and receive Your total forgiveness. As You forgive me, I choose to forgive the sins of every person who has hurt or offended me. I forgive them, give them grace, and release them to Your judgment. Holy Spirit, I pray You will help heal the pain and damage that has been done to me. Expose the enemy's lies within me. Fill me with Your grace, love, and power. In Jesus' name, amen.

Day 12

Blessing Those Who Hurt Us

There is a second step to forgiveness. First, you must bring the account to zero for everyone who has wronged you because that is what God commands. Someone might respond to this and say, "Jimmy, I've honestly tried. I pray and pray and try to forgive that person, but then nothing changes. I still feel bitter and carry all these negative emotions." Let me tell you right now, I understand that.

The man I told you I had grown to hate genuinely did and said things about me that caused great harm. He tried to orchestrate my failure, and I despised him for it. The situation was oppressive, and it went on for months. It had such a negative effect that it changed the way I interacted with Karen, my family, and other people around me. My temper grew shorter by the day, and my thoughts became darker and darker as I slid into deep bitterness and unforgiveness. I was overwhelmed, and I didn't know how to get myself out of this situation.

One day, I was praying again about this man—no, I wasn't praying about him, I was stewing about him—when the Lord nudged me and said, "Jimmy, I want you to bless that man."

That was the last thing I wanted to hear, but it was also what I needed to hear because that is how Jesus talks. He said, *"But I say to you who hear: Love your enemies, do good to those who hate you, bless those who curse you, and pray for those who spitefully use you"* (Luke 6:27–28). You may think that sounds like religious advice, but it is medicine that will heal you and change everything.

Admittedly, I heard the Lord and thought, *Lord, I'm not blessing that man. I want that man to die. I want to see his obituary. That's where my healing is going to come from.* But the Lord is the Lord, and He never changes. I would try to protest, but He just kept telling me to bless that man.

After days of avoiding what the Lord was telling me to do, I finally gave in and obeyed. On the first day, I started praying a feeble prayer for the Lord to bless the man. If I were sincere, I would have asked God to give that man what I wanted for myself, but I wasn't sincere. Even so, I would pray, "Okay then, Lord—bless him, bless his marriage, bless his children, and bless his business." But my feelings remained the same.

On the second day, I woke up and started praying and blessing that man again, but there was still no change in me. On the third day, I blessed him again. For ten days, I prayed for the Lord to bless that man. After about the tenth day of my half-hearted prayers for the man and for the Lord to help me forgive him, something happened. As I started praying again, an image came into my heart. I saw the image of a boy who was about ten years old standing outside of a house.

Immediately, I became aware that this boy had been terribly abused, and horrible things had happened to him. Then it became clear to me—I was praying for that little boy who was now that man. Once again, I began to pray for the Lord to help me forgive that man, but in my mind, I had the image of that boy. The Lord spoke to my heart and said, "Jimmy, the man that you hate is that boy. You see a man who did these terrible things to you. But I see the boy and why he did it to you." Immediately, my spiritual eyes opened, and I began to love that man. The anger and rage transformed into love and compassion.

Afterward, I didn't suddenly begin a close personal friendship with that man. He was still a difficult individual. But I never hated him again. I no longer struggled with negative thoughts. People would say to me, "Jimmy, I've prayed over and over. I've tried to forgive this person for abusing me, for rejecting me. I've tried, but nothing ever seems to change."

Let me offer my own personal testimony to you: you cannot continue hating the same person who you bless before God.

Jesus says we should bless those who curse us and pray for those who do evil against us. He teaches us that you can't fight fire with fire unless you just want a bigger fire. When you fight hate with hate, then expect more hate. If you try to fight rejection with rejection, then you'll just get more rejection. I can assure you that the only way to defeat a negative spirit in your life is with the opposite spirit. If someone did something wrong to you, then decide to go before God and bless that person. Bless until that negative spirit is off you and until the thing that person did to you is off you. Refuse retaliation, because you can't fight hate with hate. Battle curses with prayers of blessing. I can tell you from my experience, it works. It is the only thing that works.

I recognize that you may have been so deeply violated that words can't even describe the kind of devastation you have experienced. I understand that your experience is real and valid. But regardless, you simply must forgive and bless the person who hurt or offended if you are going to be healed. I have had a number of times when I had to forgive and bless someone who hurt me deeply. Even though it was difficult at the time, it produced lasting healing and freedom in my life. The same can happen for you. You know who has hurt you. Now, bless those people, and let the Lord heal your heart.

HEALING FROM GOD'S WORD

But I say to you who hear: Love your enemies, do good to those who hate you, bless those who curse you, and pray for those who spitefully use you. (Luke 6:27–28)

Therefore, as the elect of God, holy and beloved, put on tender mercies, kindness, humility, meekness, long-suffering; bearing with one another, and forgiving one another, if anyone has a complaint against another; even as Christ forgave you, so you also must do. But above all these things put on love, which is the bond of perfection. And let the peace of God rule in your hearts, to which also you were called in one body; and be thankful. (Colossians 3:12–15)

Let no corrupt word proceed out of your mouth, but what is good for necessary edification, that it may impart grace to the hearers. And do not grieve the Holy Spirit of God, by whom you were sealed for the day of redemption. Let all bitterness, wrath, anger, clamor, and evil speaking be put away from you, with all malice. And be kind to one another, tenderhearted, forgiving one another, even as God in Christ forgave you. (Ephesians 4:29–32)

HEALING TRUTHS

- God clearly commands us in His Word to forgive others. If you are a sincere believer, then you know it is true and right, but even though you may go through the motions of forgiving others many times, your feelings don't genuinely change.

- Jesus tells us to love our enemies. The word for love He uses is *agape*, which is God's kind of love that doesn't require an emotion. It is a love that proceeds from the will and seeks to do what is best for another person in the same way that God would.

- Jesus tells us to bless those who curse us and to pray for those who hurt us deeply. You will only be able to defeat a spirit with the opposite spirit. Your only other option is to respond in kind by cursing those who curse you and by doing evil to those who do evil to you, but that really doesn't solve anything. If you fight fire with fire, then you'll only get a bigger fire.

- You simply cannot hate a person for a long time when you are blessing and praying for that individual. As you are obedient to God and bless and pray for someone who hurt you, the Lord will heal your heart.

- Blessing and prayer are the opposite spirits of cursing and spitefully using others. As believers, we must not get into a tit-for-tat exchange inspired by the same spirit that exploits those who are mistreating us. We must respond differently. As you do, your behavior will become redemptive toward those who are against you. Even if it doesn't change the other person, it will protect you and keep you from being further damaged.

Exercises for Reflection and Discussion

1. Make a list of the people, past or present, whom you have tried to forgive but still have strong feelings of pain, bitterness, or anger toward them.

_____

_____

_____

_____

_____

_____

2. What are the primary ways you respond to hurtful people? Have you responded in the same spirit or with the opposite spirit?

_____

_____

_____

_____

_____

_____

3. How well do you believe you trust God fully in your relationships? Do you believe He will protect you as you trust Him, or do you believe you have to protect yourself? Explain.

_____

_____

_____

_____

_____

_____

4. What would you say is your main challenge in blessing someone who has cursed and hurt you?

_____

_____

_____

_____

_____

_____

Applying Healing Principles

Complete the following steps to apply what you have learned in the lesson:

1. **From the list you made of people you still have negative feelings toward, begin a daily practice of blessing them and praying for them by name until your emotions have been healed and changed.**

   - Some people take more time than others. On your list, put a checkmark by those with whom you believe the negative feelings have been healed. Then continue praying and checking off names until you have completed the list. You will reach a point of complete peace without any anger or bitterness remaining.

- Some people may have died since they first hurt you. Bless those people as well, and pray for them anyway. Ask the Lord to bless them and pray everything good for them and those they left behind. Do this until you are healed and can pray for them and think about them without negative feelings.

- The essence of blessing someone is to pray for them that which you would want to receive yourself. Pray for forgiveness, grace, favor, health, prosperity, promotion, and blessing upon their family. You will find this part of the process challenging. You won't want those people to have what you have or desire. You will want them to be punished, and you will want justice. Even so, God gave you grace when you were guilty and deserving of judgment. He will only give you as much grace as you are willing to give away. You cannot have grace for yourself and judgment for others. Blessing your enemies is one of the ways God will develop a true spirit of grace within you. As you give grace to your enemies, God will heal you and give you the grace you need.

2. **Ask the Holy Spirit to teach you how to respond differently to difficult people.** Pray and prepare to encounter them and change your habit patterns.

3. **Examine your emotions on a regular basis.** The primary

emotion that will tell you how you are really doing is peace. When you are at peace, you are living in the state God designed for you to live. However, if your peace is disturbed, then it is a warning signal you should heed. Anger, bitterness, anxiety, and fear are all negative emotions that you must deal with promptly and properly.

Healing Confession

Confess the following aloud:

I confess, in agreement with God's Word, that I am a child of God who has been called to live by a different spirit than that of the world. I will live by the power of the Holy Spirit and according to His nature and character. I will not respond in kind to unrighteous behavior. I will harbor neither hatred nor bitterness toward my enemies or anyone else who mistreats me. I will bless those who curse me and pray for those who mistreat me as I trust God to protect and heal me.

Healing Prayer

Silently or aloud, pray this prayer:

Holy Spirit, I commit myself to a life of grace and forgiveness. Please forgive me for the times I have responded unrighteously to hurt and offenses. Forgive me for harboring grudges and bitterness. I now willingly forgive every person who has hurt or offended me. This includes those who have hurt or offended those I love. I commit today to blessing those people and to praying for them until all hurt, bitterness, and ill will is gone. As I bless them, I pray for You to do a deep healing work in my heart. I ask you to heal all the damage that has been done within me and replace it with Your love and peace. In Jesus' name, amen.

FINAL THOUGHTS ON SECTION FIVE

The Freedom of Forgiveness

Forgiveness doesn't make the person who hurt you right, but it does make you free. When you forgive someone, it doesn't mean you excuse that individual or that their actions don't matter. Forgiveness simply means you have decided to forgive in the way that God forgave you, and you are not going to hold this offense against that person or harbor wrong emotions.

Some people say, "I keep forgiving that person, but my feelings don't change." I understand that response, but you cannot justify unforgiveness and bitterness. The damage those feelings have done in you allowed the devil to influence you as you relate to other people. You may have responded with outbursts of anger, and those actions are wrong. You must forgive every single person in your life—regardless of what they've done—to be set free and close that door on the devil.

As you go through the process of blessing people who have hurt you, things may not change immediately. It might take you a week or a month. Nevertheless, the day is coming when you will be praying, obeying God, and fighting a negative spirit with the opposite spirit, and the Lord is going to do a deep healing in your heart. It will be like draining an infection out of you. The devil will lose the open door that he has used to oppress you.

Sometimes deep discouragement, oppression, and depression come from a spirit of heaviness that the devil tries to lay on you. He uses your hurt as an open door. God, however, brings joy and peace into your life as soon as you forgive. Your prayers of blessing for another person will bless you. You are sowing good seed, and you are going to reap good in return. I encourage you to never again allow unforgiveness, bitterness, or any other negative emotion to take residence inside you. Don't let it stay because it's only going to hurt you. Forgive people, bless them, and pray for them until God heals your heart and sets you free.

SECTION SIX

OVERCOMING SHAME

Genesis chapter 2 has one of the most beautiful passages in the Bible. God created a perfect paradise and placed two humans in it. They were perfect in their bodies, and they were naked without shame (see Genesis 2:25). Can you imagine living in a world with neither shame nor condemnation? Both emotions damage us. When God approached Adam and Eve after they sinned, they were ashamed (see Genesis 3:9–11). Before they sinned, they were completely emotionally healthy and free, as God created them to be until the devil and sin entered the picture. As soon as Adam and Eve disobeyed God, the devil put shame upon them to separate them from God and each other as he does to all of us when we fail or experience hurt. However, God can heal the feelings of shame and condemnation in your life.

Day 13

The Burden of Shame

The thing about shame is there's often no specific reason for it. Imagine I am driving on the road, and a police officer pulls me over. He approaches the drivers' side of my car and says, "Mr. Evans, I clocked you going 75 in a 60-mile-per-hour zone. I'm going to issue you a ticket for the violation." As a result, I pay my fine and that is it. It's specifically related to my violation of the law and isn't personal. Imagine again I am traveling on the road, and the same officer stops me. This time he walks to my window and says, "First of all, you're ugly. I can't stand the way you look. You even smell bad. Second, you're the worst driver I've ever seen in my entire life. You're just terrible. I've been watching you drive, and you're just no good. In fact, you're not even a good person. Now, get out of here!"

What am I supposed to do with that second encounter with the officer? He didn't even name a specific violation. He didn't like me. He said I'm not good. I didn't get a ticket, but I still had an awful feeling when he left. Condemnation and shame are like the second time I was pulled over. They come into our lives, and offer us no method of resolution. You see, I can pay the fine. If you tell me something specific that I did wrong, I can deal with that. But if I pay a fine for the second stop, then what am I paying it for, and how much is it? The only thing I know is the officer thinks I'm a failure. Whenever you get these kinds of feelings about vague accusations you can't do anything about, then you can always know they came straight from the devil.

The Holy Spirit doesn't operate that way. He is gentle, wonderful, and extremely specific. We are saved by grace, and there's no condemnation. In fact, the apostle Paul says, *"There is therefore now no condemnation to those who are in Christ Jesus, who do not walk according to the flesh, but according to the spirit"* (Romans 8:1). This passage means that if God wanted to condemn us, then Jesus wouldn't have died to pay for our sins. Everything God does in our lives, He does by grace and not according to a point system. We don't have to do anything to deserve God's love and acceptance. He gives us His favor freely; it is a gift of grace. Although we've all done things God doesn't like, it doesn't change His love for us, and He never rejects us.

God always wants to have a relationship with you.

He's madly in love with you. He made you in your mother's womb, not as an afterthought, accident, or mistake, but as the handiwork of the living God (see Psalm 139). When the Holy

Spirit is doing something in your life, He will speak to your heart very gently and very specifically something like, "Hey, next time you talk to that person, be more positive. Don't use that kind of language. I love you. Just use better language."

The devil tries to deliver a vastly different message. He will say something like, You're no good. You're ugly. I don't like you. God doesn't like you. You do the same thing over and over and even though you keep telling God you're going to change, you don't change. You're such a spiritually low-class person. You might squeak into heaven, but God doesn't love you as much as other people. You're just not a good person. In fact, you're defective and broken. Something's wrong with you. You better keep your distance from God." This is how the devil works. He is on both sides of sin's door. On one side, he tempts us to sin, and on the other, he condemns us when we do. He stood on one side in the Garden of Eden and tempted Adam and Eve. As soon as they sinned, the devil was there with condemnation, guilt, and shame.

In God's eyes, our righteousness is nothing but filthy rags (see Isaiah 64:6). All of us have fallen short of the glory of God (see Romans 3:23). Even so, there is no condemnation because Jesus died for our sins. I'm the righteousness of God in Christ, even when I'm not doing the best I can, or I'm making a mistake (see 2 Corinthians 5:21). You may have been raised in a home with parents who shamed you. They never said things like, "Bobby, next time, would you clean up your room better? You can do better than that." Instead, they said, "You're lazy, no good, and you'll never be good." They used shame both to correct and to punish you for something you did wrong. You always felt as if you never measured up. I knew an adult man in his fifties who was emotionally devastated because, when he was a boy, his father came to him one day and said, "You're no good. You never will be any good. You'll never succeed in life." After 40 years, this man was still devastated because of that feeling of shame and condemnation that had destroyed his sense of self-worth.

I want you to know that whatever someone else said to you to put shame and condemnation on you, it did not come from your heavenly Father. I urge you to take those thoughts captive and replace them with what God's Word says about you: you're the righteousness of God in Christ. That's what the Bible says about you. God accepts you, and you are His beloved. There is no condemnation for you. You have been forgiven. God created you in your mother's womb, and your birthright in Christ is victory and success. If He wants to correct something in your life, then He will do it by His grace, very specifically.

I love that the Holy Spirit comes to us and says, "Hey, you did this thing." Then, He helps us overcome by His power and grace. Condemnation only points its finger at you and tells you how wrong you are, but there's no help in condemnation; that's just the devil talking, trying to tear you down, so you never become who God wants you to be. However, when God's grace comes to you, He tells you what you're doing wrong, and He helps you change without condemnation or shame. You can overcome condemnation and shame by replacing them with God's thoughts about you.

HEALING FROM GOD'S WORD

There is therefore now no condemnation to those who are in Christ Jesus, who do not walk according to the flesh, but according to the Spirit. For the law of the Spirit of life in Christ Jesus has made me free from the law of sin and death. For what the law could not do in that it was weak through the flesh, God did by sending His own Son in the likeness of sinful flesh, on account of sin: He condemned sin in the flesh, that the righteous requirement of the law might be fulfilled in us who do not walk according to the flesh but according to the Spirit. (Romans 8:1–4)

As it is written: "Behold, I lay in Zion a stumbling stone and rock of offense, And whoever believes on Him will not be put to shame." (Romans 9:33)

The Lord is merciful and gracious,
Slow to anger, and abounding in mercy.
He will not always strive with us,
Nor will He keep His anger forever.

He has not dealt with us according to our sins,
Nor punished us according to our iniquities.
For as the heavens are high above the earth,
So great is His mercy toward those who fear Him;
As far as the east is from the west,
So far has He removed our transgressions from us.
As a father pities his children,
So the Lord pities those who fear Him.
For He knows our frame;
He remembers that we are dust. (Psalm 103:8–14)

For you did not receive the spirit of bondage again to fear, but you received the Spirit of adoption by whom we cry out, "Abba, Father." (Romans 8:15)

Love has been perfected among us in this: that we may have boldness in the day of judgment; because as He is, so are we in this world. There is no fear in love; but perfect love casts out fear, because fear involves torment. But he who fears has not been made perfect in love. We love Him because He first loved us. (1 John 4:17–19)

HEALING TRUTHS

- The devil doesn't want you to be in a relationship with God or other people. He will do whatever he can to cause disunity in your relationships so he can keep you isolated and defeated. Shame and condemnation are two of the main tools he uses to drive us apart.

- With shame and condemnation, you cannot identify a specific issue to address, so you have no way to deal with it. *All shame and condemnation are of the devil!* God will *never* use shame or condemnation against you. If you want to be healed and set free, then you must see shame and condemnation for what they are: enemy agents to reject in Jesus' name.

- The Holy Spirit will always be gentle and extremely specific when He is dealing with you about sin or something else He wants to correct. If what you are experiencing isn't loving and specific, then you can be sure it isn't God.

- The Holy Spirit will specifically convict you of those things He wants you to confess, correct, improve, or change. He is there to help and not hurt you. The Holy Spirit isn't a legalistic parent who will yell at you and demand for you to change on your own. He speaks for a precious, loving Father who will specifically tell you what He wants you to do, then give you the power to do it. He loves being a Father to you. He isn't the least bit bothered by your need for His help. In fact, He loves it. He wants you to invite Him into every problem, struggle, weakness, and battle with sin. He is on your side.

- The devil wants to access the hurts and failures of your past so he can put shame and condemnation on you. It is easier for him to do this if you have come out of an environment that was characterized by performance and shame. He will try to find an opportunity in every moral failure, physical flaw, inability, difficulty, chronic sin, broken relationship, financial problem, or negative life issue. He is an expert at finding them. When he attacks you, he will never appear as the devil—at least not at first. He uses stealth and cunning to whisper words into your mind and heart, and then he slithers away, leaving a path of destruction behind him. At best, you are left holding thoughts of shame and condemnation, all the while thinking that you produced those feelings on your own. At worst, he tries to make you think those ideas came from God. Nevertheless, the devil has already lost the battle. Jesus' blood has cleansed your sins, so you are now free forever from the tyranny of shame and condemnation.

Exercises for Reflection and Discussion

1. List the areas of your life where you battle with shame and condemnation.

_____

_____

_____

_____

_____

_____

2. Which people or institutions in your past used shame and condemnation as an attempt to get you to change or to make you feel bad?

_____

_____

_____

_____

_____

_____

3. What were the times in your life when you did not believe the blood of Jesus had forgiven you completely? When have you not believed God completely accepts you as you are? Describe your struggles with those issues.

_____

_____

_____

_____

_____

_____

4. What open doors has the devil used in your life to place shame and condemnation on you? Examples might include sin, your appearance, a moral failure or someone's words.

_____

_____

_____

_____

_____

_____

Applying Healing Principles

Complete the following steps to apply what you have learned in the lesson:

1. **Forgive your parents or anyone else who has used shame or condemnation to control or manipulate you.** As you go through this process, disassociate their behavior and example from God. Then tell God that you know He doesn't

operate like people do. Praise Him for His grace and for the blood of Jesus that has totally erased your sins.

2. **Forgive yourself for any of the sins of your past that the devil still tries to use to shame or condemn you.** You might be struggling with the aftereffects of an abortion, an affair, a crime, a bondage, or another sinful action. There is no sin that God refuses to forgive, and when God forgives, He forgets. (See Psalm 103) Constant regret and guilt for your past is another form of condemnation. You must forgive yourself, learn from your mistakes, accept God's forgiveness, and move on.

3. **When you struggle with thoughts of shame or condemnation, realize that they are of the devil and then address him directly.** Instead of wrestling with these thoughts or wondering if they are from God, say something such as, "Devil, I bind you in Jesus' name, and I reject every thought of shame and condemnation you are trying to put in my mind right now. I am saved and forgiven by the blood of Jesus, and God totally accepts me as I am right now. Now, I thank You, Jesus, for Your blood that covers me and makes me acceptable to You." That is the way you deal with shame and condemnation. You must make it personal between you and the enemy and defeat him by faith in the grace of Jesus and in His blood.

4. **Recognize that one of the reasons the devil uses shame and condemnation is that it makes the issue about you and not about God.** In a way, shame and condemnation can become another form of pride because they are self-focused. Grace, however, is not about us; it is about Jesus. That is the reason you must not allow the devil to make it about you. One of the best ways for you to combat shame and condemnation is to praise and worship God for His love and grace. Refuse to allow the devil to make it about you, and every time he tries, turn it into a worship service. The devil hates to hear God praised, and he especially hates hearing about the blood of Jesus because that is what defeated him.

Healing Confession

Confess the following aloud:
I confess, in agreement with God's Word, that I have been saved, forgiven, and adopted into the family of God by the blood of Jesus and by His grace. The blood of Jesus is stronger than any sin, mistake, or problem I have in my life. God completely accepts me and loves me. I now renounce all shame and condemnation in my life and know that it is of the devil. I will not allow the devil to make it about me and what I have done, who I am, or what I haven't done right. It is about God and His grace. It is about how the love of God has saved and redeemed me, despite my failures. From this day forward, I will live by grace, with my eyes on Jesus.

Healing Prayer

Silently or aloud, pray this prayer:

Father in Heaven, I come to You today as my loving Dad, and I am so thankful for who You are in my life. I will never again believe that You don't love me or that You are against me. I pray that Your name will be hallowed in my life and that I will see You for who You really are. I pray that You will help me grow in Your grace and my understanding of Your love. I ask for total healing in my relationship with You.

Holy Spirit, teach me how to walk by grace and depend upon You with neither shame nor condemnation. In Jesus' name, amen.

FINAL THOUGHTS ON SECTION SIX

God's Love is the Cure

Shame and condemnation damage your sense of self-esteem and make you think too lowly of yourself, which leads to humiliation and low self-esteem. You need to love yourself and think highly of yourself because God created you, and His love is the cure to that damage. You are the righteousness of God in Christ and a member of God's family. He fashioned you in your mother's womb, and though we may make mistakes, *He doesn't.*

If there is something God really wants to do in your life, He will do it through love and grace, by revealing specific truths and giving you the power to overcome issues in your life. God is your best friend, and He acts like your best friend. He will never use shame and condemnation with you. When you sense condemnation, come against it in the name of Jesus. Stand up against it and counter it with the truth of God's Word. The truth of the Bible is going to heal you on the inside, and it's going to change the way you think about yourself. Once you begin to walk in God's love and grace, the next time condemnation tries to creep into your thoughts, you will quickly recognize it and know that it came from the devil.

SECTION SEVEN

CONFRONTING FEAR

If we want to be healed, then we have to recognize that some of the things that ail us do not begin within us; they come from outside of us. Fear is one of those problems that often comes from an outside source that we aren't aware of.

A normal, healthy kind of fear might happen if someone was lunging at you with a knife. In that case, it's good for you to be aware and alert and get out of the way. Or if you're driving down the road, and someone swerves into your lane, then a healthy fear will cause you to move your car to avoid a collision.

But there is also an unhealthy, demonic type of fear. When you meet tragedy in your life, endure hurt, or face failure, the devil will try to use those experiences to embed a spirit of fear. This is not the natural fear of facing something that threatens your life. A good, natural fear comes with a threat and goes away when the threat is removed. Demonic fear, however, comes and stays; it is persistent and debilitating. God wants to deliver you from debilitating, chronic fear.

You could have a fear of financial failure, illness, death, or even people. Several years ago, I read a book called *When People Are Big and God is Small: Overcoming Peer Pressure, Codependency, and the Fear of Man* by Edward T. Welch. That title describes the fear of man perfectly. When you're walking in the fear of man, what people think means everything, and what God thinks doesn't mean a whole lot. You keep doing what you're doing, not because you want to do it or because you think it's the right thing to do, but because you want to be accepted by other people and gain their approval. You might gain some small measure of satisfaction, but it is coupled with the constant fear of disapproval. You terrorize yourself, thinking you're going to do something to disappoint them, and then they will reject you. You might keep your teeth gleaming white, work out for six-pack abs, drive the right car, wear the right clothes, and say the right things, but you're in a performance-based relationship. In the end, they will probably reject you at some point anyway. When you live in the fear of man, rejection is absolutely devastating. God wants to free you from the fear of man and every other type of fear the devil tries to put on you.

Day 14

Recognizing the Spirit of Fear

The writer of Hebrews says that the fear of death is how Satan controls people (see Hebrews 2:14–15). The truth is, however, that though believers die, death does not have victory over us. If you're a believer, there is never an instant in time that death will have authority over you. Even so, the devil will try to use the fear of death to paralyze you. Other common fears the devil uses are rejection and failure.

Demonic fear is different from healthy fear because it doesn't pass with the danger; it stays. With demonic fear comes the overwhelming, impending sense that another shoe is going to drop. There's also the feeling that just around the corner, the damage that happened to you in the past will reoccur soon. Failure is just on the other side of your next success. Or a bad future is going to eclipse your good present. I refer to demonic fear as a "prophet spirit." It gives us a negative report about the future, so we will make fear-based decisions that don't take God's love or power into account.

God never honors fear-based decisions.

I can testify that the biggest regrets I have in life are from when I made decisions based on fear. They were never right. In fact, they often caused some of my greatest fears to come true. You might fear financial failure, so then you make a fear-based decision, and you lose money. You might fear someone's rejection, so you relate to that person based on your insecurities, which then leads them to reject you. Your fears will cause what you fear to happen.

If you know you want to live by faith, trust in God's love, and believe what the Bible teaches, then let your will override your emotions, so you don't act on fear. I want you to see fear as an outside entity that's not a part of you—you can overcome it. As I have said several times, the devil is cunning and stealthy. He slithered into the Garden of Eden in the form of a serpent because he didn't want Adam or Eve to recognize who he really was.

The devil wants you to think that fear is an essential part of you, but the apostle Paul plainly says, *"God has not given us a spirit of fear, but of power and of love and of a sound mind"* (2 Timothy 1:7). Understand that when you're dealing with fear, you're dealing with a spirit, but it didn't come from God. God's Spirit, the Holy Spirit, doesn't use fear to control us. Quite the opposite, His language is love.

The spirit of fear may come upon you because of something someone said to you, something from your past, a failure, a sin, or something like that. The devil uses those experiences and emotions as open doors. I'm not saying you're demon-possessed—because you're not—but in those moments, a demonic spirit of fear is whispering lies to you that produce this negative emotion. Fear is a remarkably high consumer of our emotions. When you live in long-term fear, you will eventually become discouraged and even depressed because it wears out your emotions and drains you the same way anger does. The only way forward is for you to see fear as an outside entity. It's not you, and God didn't give it to you. My hope is that you will learn to rise up and take authority over it.

HEALING FROM GOD'S WORD

You will keep him in perfect peace,
Whose mind is stayed on You,
Because he trusts in You. (Isaiah 26:3)

Behold, I give you the authority to trample on serpents
and scorpions, and over all the power of the enemy, and
nothing shall by any means hurt you. (Luke 10:19)

Be anxious for nothing, but in everything by prayer
and supplication, with thanksgiving, let your requests

be made known to God; and the peace of God, which surpasses all understanding, will guard your hearts and minds through Christ Jesus. (Philippians 4:6–7)

He who dwells in the secret place of the Most High
Shall abide under the shadow of the Almighty.
I will say of the Lord, "He is my refuge and my fortress;
My God, in Him I will trust."
Surely He shall deliver you from the snare of the fowler
And from the perilous pestilence.
He shall cover you with His feathers,
And under His wings you shall take refuge;
His truth shall be your shield and buckler.
You shall not be afraid of the terror by night,
Nor of the arrow that flies by day,
Nor of the pestilence that walks in darkness,
Nor of the destruction that lays waste at noonday.
A thousand may fall at your side,
And ten thousand at your right hand;
But it shall not come near you.
Only with your eyes shall you look,
And see the reward of the wicked.
Because you have made the Lord, who is my refuge,
Even the Most High, your dwelling place,
No evil shall befall you,
Nor shall any plague come near your dwelling;
For He shall give His angels charge over you,

To keep you in all your ways.
In their hands they shall bear you up,
Lest you dash your foot against a stone.
You shall tread upon the lion and the cobra,
The young lion and the serpent you shall trample
underfoot.
"Because he has set his love upon Me, therefore I will
deliver him;
I will set him on high, because he has known My name.
He shall call upon Me, and I will answer him;
I will be with him in trouble;
I will deliver him and honor him.
With long life I will satisfy him,
And show him My salvation." (Psalm 91:1–16)

HEALING TRUTHS

- There are two types of fear: healthy fear and chronic, debilitating fear. God programmed a healthy fear into us to keep us safe, which includes fear of harmful animals and insects, fear of heights, and the urge to flee dangerous situations. We need to have this type of fear. However, some fear comes to us through demonic influence. It can range from low-grade anxiety to hysteria. The difference between this and the first type of fear is that it isn't designed to save or help us. It does the opposite. It

consumes our mental and emotional energy and ulti-
mately brings about the results we fear will happen. Even
if nothing ever happens, we constantly live in the shadow
of that fear.

- Some of our fears are based on what we don't understand.
  But once we have knowledge, our fears decrease. If you
  struggle with fear in any area, then make sure you counter
  it with knowledge. An example is marriage. Many people
  in our society fear it because of all of the problems they
  see or have experienced. But they fear it because they
  don't understand it. You have a 100% chance of success
  in marriage when you do it God's way. You just need to
  understand it. Our ministry, XO Marriage, exists to help
  people thrive in marriage and we see couples go from
  the brink of divorce to being deeply in love all of the time.
  They are good people, but they struggle because of ignorance. They just need the right information.

- The devil wants to use our fallen emotions to entrench a
  spirit of fear within us. He uses any negative emotion for
  this purpose, but his main strategy is to use trauma and
  pain. Many of your worst fears stem from the trauma of
  your past. When you go through something that hurts or
  traumatizes you, the experience may open a door to the
  devil. Only when you turn to the Lord and put your faith
  in Him does the door close.

- Fear is a "prophet spirit" with hellish origins, meaning it gives a negative report about the future. A spirit of fear constantly plays on your fears to keep you upset. The devil designed this kind of fear to influence you to make fear-based decisions that won't honor God. The Lord does not bless fear-based decisions. He only rewards faith!

- Jesus has defeated the devil and given us authority. We need to use it to uncover the enemy's tricks and bind him in Jesus' name. We are not helpless victims; we are the bride of Christ and children of the Most High God. He wants us to act like we believe those things about ourselves, to rise up against fear and overcome it.

Exercises for Reflection and Discussion

1. Make a list of traumatic events in your past that the devil tried to use to implant a spirit of fear within you?

_____

_____

_____

_____

_____

2. Make a list of your main fears.

_____

_____

_____

_____

_____

_____

3. Would you say your main fears are based on ignorance or a spirit of fear? Explain.

_____

_____

_____

_____

_____

_____

4. How has fear kept you from obeying God and putting your trust in Him?

_____

_____

_____

_____

_____

_____

Applying Healing Principles

Complete the following steps to apply what you have learned in the lesson:

1. **From the list of your main fears, call each fear by name and take authority over it in Jesus' name.** Command it to be bound and cast it out. Go through your full list. You may pray a prayer such as this:

    Spirit of fear, I bind you in Jesus' name and by the power of His blood. I command you to lose your hold on me right now. I cast you out of my life, and I replace you with faith in God and His Word. Never again will I listen to you or allow you to upset me or direct my life. You have lost your place in me, and I command you to leave now. In Jesus' name, amen.

    Say that prayer every time fear tries to influence or harass you, and you will win over it. As a believer in Jesus Christ, you carry His authority, and the devil knows it.

2. **Set your will over your emotions.** Our soul holds our will and emotions, but our emotions must not rule over our will because they are prone to demonic attack. When you confront fear, in particular, your emotions may be real, but that doesn't mean they are right or helpful. When you set your will over your emotions, you choose not to allow your fears to control you. You can still admit your fear to God, and you should, since He already knows it is there. As you acknowledge your fear, however, tell the Lord that you are committed to doing what is right. Then ask the Holy Spirit for power, love, and a sound mind, in accordance with 2 Timothy 1:7, and He will give it to you. When you act in faith, you will overcome your fears and bring your dreams into reality. I have been confronted with many strong and very demonic fears in my life. Even though they seem very real and powerful at the time, they all die, one step of faith at a time.

3. **Meditate on this saying: fear is expecting the devil to act, and faith is expecting God to act.** Faith or fear will arise within us based on where we place our focus: God or the devil; good or bad; faith or fear.

Healing Confession

Confess the following aloud:
I confess, in agreement with God's Word, that I have the

authority of Jesus Christ over all the enemy's power, which includes a spirit of fear that would come to harass and intimidate me. I take authority over every spirit of fear in my life in Jesus' name. I will not cower to fear any longer or allow it to control my thoughts or actions. By an act of my will, I choose faith over fear. I will subject my emotions to my will and live by faith in God's Word.

Healing Prayer

Silently or aloud, pray this prayer:

In the name of Jesus, I take authority over every demonic spirit of fear that has come into my life. However, or wherever you gained entry, I close the door on you now and cast you out. I uncover you and all the thoughts and feelings you incite within me. You are here to keep me from knowing and trusting in God. You are here to keep me upset so I will continue to make fear-based decisions that keep me failing, frustrated, and fearful. For those reasons, I reject you and cast you out. I choose faith in God over you, and from this day forward, I will put my faith in God.

Holy Spirit, in the place of my fears, I pray You will give me love, power, and a sound mind. I put my trust in You and thank You for my new freedom. Heal me completely of all the damage that fear has done to me and fill me with Your peace. Heal all the trauma and pain the devil used as his access points into my life. In Jesus' name, amen.

Day 15

No Longer Fear People

I counseled a woman one time who had been shamed earlier in her life. She was a beautiful woman, but she had a cruel and abusive father who delighted in publicly disgracing her, and it caused her great damage. Through the pain and humiliation of her past, she lived every moment of every day to satisfy other people. She dressed to please them and talked and acted in a manner that was not natural for her. This woman wasn't herself or her own person—in fact, she wasn't even sure who she really was. She couldn't disagree with anyone or do anything she thought would cause disapproval. This woman was in constant bondage to the fear of other people. Even worse, she constantly feared she was going to fail others until it finally consumed her. She then had a complete mental and emotional breakdown. Her healing began when she realized she couldn't please or appease everyone.

Jesus responds to our fear of people by saying, *"Beware when all men speak well of you"* (Luke 6:26, my paraphrase). He, more than anyone else, understands the truth of the saying, "You can't please everyone." Our number one fear—a holy fear—should be of God. He's the primary one we should concern ourselves with pleasing. The fear of God is different from demonic fear or even healthy fear; it is a divine respect for Him. We should wonder first what He thinks about what we are doing before we ever consider anyone else's thoughts. God loves us, and He is exceedingly powerful, which means we need to understand people are extremely small in comparison. The prophet Jeremiah quotes the Lord, saying, *"Cursed is the man who trusts in man and makes flesh his strength"* (Jeremiah 17:5). Our strength is in the Lord, and any other pretense of power is cursed.

When I first entered the ministry, the church where I was the pastor had about 900 members, and I lived in constant fear of failure and rejection. I admit my focus was not solely on God. I focused on preaching, but I always had the concern of people liking me at the front of my mind. I thought about whether they were giving to the church or if the church was succeeding and growing. I lived in the fear of man, and it was consuming me. Even worse, it almost ruined my marriage. I frittered away a couple of especially important years of my relationship with my children because what people thought about me was eating me alive. I concentrated on how I looked and on doing everything right. People became big, and God became small until one day, I woke up. I was just completely worn out by it all, and the results of my actions were telling on me. I realized that I wasn't my own person. I wasn't even doing the things I liked to do. I was spending my time doing what I thought people wanted me to do and doing my best to pretend that I liked it.

On that day, the Lord revealed my mistake, and I said, "You know something, Lord? I repent because you have become small in my life. I confess pleasing others is not the right thing I should care about. I've mainly been doing things to get the approval of people." I realized I was living in sin—not in the way most people think about sin.

A few summers ago, I took my grandkids to the swimming pool. There was a woman with a tattoo on her back. This kind of tattoo was immensely popular 10 or more years ago. I overheard two other women making fun of it, saying it was outdated. My point is that what people loved you for 10 years ago, now they've suddenly changed their minds about. You will wear yourself out trying to chase that kind of fickle approval.

God does not change in His love for you. He will never reject you, leave you, or forsake you.

God is your absolute best friend. He's madly in love with you just the way you are right now. God is the one we should care most about. He will be with you 24 hours a day, seven days a week. Eternally, His opinion is going to make the biggest difference in your life, but today, His blessing is the most important thing and not the approval of people. The fear of man creates bondage, but God gives freedom.

HEALING FROM GOD'S WORD

Woe to you when all men speak well of you,
For so did their fathers to the false prophets. (Luke 6:26)

For whoever is ashamed of Me and My words in this
adulterous and sinful generation, of him the Son of Man
also will be ashamed when He comes in the glory of His
Father with the holy angels. (Mark 8:38)

Thus says the Lord:
"Cursed is the man who trusts in man
And makes flesh his strength,
Whose heart departs from the Lord.
For he shall be like a shrub in the desert,
And shall not see when good comes,
But shall inhabit the parched places in the wilderness,
In a salt land which is not inhabited.
Blessed is the man who trusts in the Lord,
And whose hope is the Lord.
For he shall be like a tree planted by the waters,
Which spreads out its roots by the river,
And will not fear when heat comes;
But its leaf will be green,
And will not be anxious in the year of drought,
Nor will cease from yielding fruit." (Jeremiah 17:5–8)

Therefore do not worry, saying, "What shall we eat?" or "What shall we drink?" or "What shall we wear?" For after all these things the Gentiles seek. For your heavenly Father knows that you need all these things. But seek first the kingdom of God and His righteousness, and all these things shall be added to you. (Matthew 6:31–33)

HEALING TRUTHS

- When our focus is on people rather than on God, they become idols to us. We worship their approval and go to extremes to gain it, and then we make every effort not to lose it. Because our focus is on the endorsement of people, we say things we don't mean, do things we really don't want to do, and even worse, we compromise our morals and core beliefs.

- In some cases, we are raised in homes that do not put God first. Our parents did not focus on receiving His blessing; they concentrated on getting ahead. Because that was the center of their attention, we were, in turn, trained to please the "right" people as an essential element of our survival.

- Our contemporary culture is obsessed with appearance, position, wealth, and political correctness. It is as if we are subject to an invisible scorecard by which we are constantly measured. We do everything we can to look better, appear richer, and gain position by saying and doing the things we think are acceptable. However, when we jockey for appearance and performance, it is a charade, a farce, and a cruel lie. Look closely, and you will see that those who have reached the top of the ladder are in many cases not genuinely happy. In fact, people at the top are often some of the most miserable people on earth.

- Why do we try so hard to gain things so people will approve of us? We feel enormous pressure, and it doesn't really make us happy. We strive, work, perform, and compromise to get the approval of people and to acquire the things we think will make us acceptable to them. Once we reach our intended destination, we realize we haven't arrived on a mountaintop of success at all; instead, we have entered a prison of performance. You might have earned six-pack abs, bleached your teeth until they're stunningly white, and have the hair of a model, but you'd better not lose any of them because you will risk losing the approval they helped you gain. The same lips that praised you for looking so good will mock you when you inevitably disappoint them.

- Only God and the blessing you receive from Him will ever make you genuinely happy in life. When He is in your life and blessing you, you will find that it really doesn't matter what the wrong people think. God doesn't distribute His love based on your performance. His Word never commands you to pile up a certain amount of money, attain the perfect physique, or do anything else to gain the approval of people.

- The Bible never offers much of a description for Jesus' appearance because it doesn't really matter. We love Him because of His character, not His looks. He was raised in the home of a humble craftsman, a carpenter and builder. He came from a normal small town, yet He was the most extraordinary person who will ever live. Jesus' own people rejected Him, even though He loved them and tried to help them. He didn't fit their expectations because He didn't have the accepted pedigree for the religious establishment's approval. He wasn't wealthy enough to buy into their corrupt system, and if He had been, He still wouldn't have done it. Jesus refused to live to fit in. As followers of Jesus, we know it is a sin for us to compromise our faith in Him to gain the approval of people.

- Throughout life's journey, you are bound to disappoint someone along the way. You must choose what kind of person you will be. Will you disappoint God by chasing after the approval of people over pursuing a relationship with Him, or are you willing to disappoint some people as you choose God? What you choose will make all the difference in your life.

Exercises for Reflection and Discussion

1. Would you say you are controlled or even greatly influenced by your fear of other people? If so, explain.

_____

_____

_____

_____

_____

2. Does the fear of man cause you to compromise your relationship with God? If so, how is this true?

_____

_____

_____

_____

_____

_____

3. Are there people in your life that you fear disappointing, or do you feel deep anxiety if you have to say "no," to them? If so, who are those people?

_____

_____

_____

_____

_____

_____

4. What is the main fear you have regarding disappointing people?

_____

_____

_____

_____

_____

_____

Applying Healing Principles

Complete the following steps to apply what you have learned in the lesson:

1. **If you realized you have focused more on pleasing people than on pleasing God, then repent to Him for the sin of fearing man.** As you tell the Lord you want to change your heart, mind, and actions, ask Him to give you the power to stand up to people in a loving way and to stand up for your faith with boldness.

2. **Ask the Holy Spirit to show you if there are wounds from rejection or key painful moments in your life that have caused you to fear people in a wrong way.** As you do so, ask Him to heal your self-esteem and any other areas of your life that the enemy uses to influence you. You may have an unhealthy fear of man because your self-esteem is damaged, and your focus is not on who God says you are. Never allow your self-esteem to be based primarily on your appearance, possessions, status, or what other people think about you. Your self-esteem is based on the fact that God formed you in your mother's womb as His special and unique child. Even though the world may conditionally love you based on its superficial values, God loves you unconditionally because you are His.

3. **Make a list of the people or the types of people you fear the most.** Pray over the list as you ask the Holy Spirit to heal you of any fears you have related to this list. Also, ask Him to give you boldness and confidence to be yourself while still being loving and righteous. Ask Him to help you have a willingness to be ok with being judged or rejected by those you fear.

4. **Take authority over the fear of man in Jesus' name.** The spirit of fear comes from the devil (see 2 Timothy 1:7), and it incites us to rebel against God. You must address fear as an entity and not just an emotion. It is an enemy that the devil has sent to destroy your life, and you must see it as such.

Healing Confession

Confess the following aloud:

I confess, in agreement with God's Word, that God is first in my life. I care most about what He says and about His blessing. God's presence is what makes me happy and fulfilled. His love is based on grace and not on performance. He will never reject me or put pressure on me to do something I shouldn't do. I am willing to lose the approval of people, but I am unwilling to lose God's approval. From this point forward, my focus is on God and not on the approval of people.

Healing Prayer

Silently or aloud, pray this prayer:

Holy Spirit, I ask you to heal any part of me that has been hurt or damaged by the past. This includes training from my parents, peer pressure, and the rejection of people I didn't please, among other hurts. I want my heart to be healthy and whole, so I will not be controlled or tormented by what people think. I also want to be able to love people and be an example for them, despite what they think about me or my faith in Christ. Give me supernatural boldness and confidence concerning my faith in Christ and who I am in You. I pray that You will heal my self-esteem and help me to have God-confidence rather than mere self-confidence. I pray all of this in Jesus' name, amen.

FINAL THOUGHTS ON SECTION SEVEN

Faith Over Fear

As I said previously, some fear is healthy and normal. In fact, God has given it to you to help you in a time of crisis and keep you safe. However, demonic fear never leaves you. It may manifest in anxiety or terror, but it also consumes your life, causes you to make poor decisions, and harms your relationship with God and others. God wants you to have power, love, and a sound mind so you can live by faith, do the right things, and not be driven by a spirit of fear.

You might say, "But Jimmy, I have a lot of fear." I am telling you that you are not a fearful person. That is not you; it's a spirit of fear. Jesus told us that we have authority over the enemy: *"Behold, I have given you authority to tread on serpents and scorpions, and over all the power of the enemy, and nothing will injure you."* (Luke 10:19).

You may also struggle with the fear of man or of people. I want everyone to like me, but I recognize not everyone will. I think I'm a good and godly person, and I treat everyone right, but some people are just not going to like who I am. They may not accept that I'm a Christian or like how I look or talk—that fact used to devastate and consume me. I lived in fear of man.

Back then, I wasn't the person I wanted to be. I compromised so much of myself for the sake of other people. In the end, I was left full of frustration and failure until I repented for caring more about what people thought than I did about what God thought. People in my life had become idols. God was small, and people were big. Then I came to the end of myself and repented. God became big, and I had the right perspective of people in my life. As a result, I experienced freedom.

SECTION EIGHT

THE CURE FOR JEALOUSY AND ENVY

When we have been hurt or damaged inside, jealousy and envy become part of our lives. The apostle Paul told the Galatian believers that jealousy and envy are works of the flesh (see Galatians 5:19–21). All of us become naturally jealous and envious at some point in our lives. Perhaps you struggle with one or both emotions. They are normal, and we must manage them properly. However, if they become consuming, they will wear you out to the point you cannot rest. You will find yourself constantly vigilant to make sure no one has things better than you have. At that point, jealousy and envy become sinful and destructive.

Day 16

An Orphan Spirit

Are jealousy and envy the same thing? No, they are different. Generally speaking, jealousy is about people, and envy is about things. Jealousy says, "I'm jealous about your relationship with someone else." Envy says, "I am bothered that you have something I don't have." Envy is almost always wrong, but jealousy can sometimes be good.

In Exodus, God says, *"My name is Jealous. I'm a jealous God"* (Exodus 34:14, my paraphrase). If jealousy were always wrong, then God wouldn't be jealous. Jealousy, under control, protects the integrity of a relationship. For example, if I were flirting with another female, I expect my wife would get jealous. That's a good thing. She's protecting the integrity of our relationship. (For the record, I wouldn't try it, and I wouldn't recommend you do it either.)

But if I am jealous of a relationship that does not belong to me—for example, another man's wife—then that is bad jealousy. I would be wanting something I should not have. Or I could want someone else's possessions that I can't get for whatever reason, and I become envious and adversarial with that person. That is envy, and it is wrong. The Pharisees turned Jesus over to be killed because they were envious (see Matthew 27:18). Pontius Pilate even noted the Pharisees were envious. Why were they envious? Was it because of Jesus' popularity? He was extremely popular with the people, and the Pharisees became envious of that to the point that they wanted Him dead. Jealousy and envy can cause us to do some very wrong things, up to and including murder.

How, then, should you manage jealousy and envy when you feel those emotions? As Paul says, you have to first recognize that they are deeds of the flesh (see Galatians 5:19–21). All of us can experience jealousy and envy at any point in time. The answer for you when you encounter those emotions is the Holy Spirit. In fact, Paul says the answer to emotions such as envy is the fruit of the Spirit: *"But the fruit of the Spirit is love, joy, peace, patience, kindness, goodness, faithfulness, gentleness, self-control"* (Galatians 5:22–23, NASB). If you deal with jealousy or envy, then you must understand that it is part of your default setting to operate in the flesh. Nevertheless, God calls you to operate in the Spirit. He designed you to work that way under the Holy Spirit's power inside you. When you experience feelings of jealousy and envy, say, "Holy Spirit, I'm feeling jealous right now. I'm feeling envious right now. I come to you in honesty and ask you to fill me with the fruit of the Spirit."

The second thing you should do is *go to your heavenly Father* with your needs. God is your Father, and He cares about you. Jesus taught His followers to pray, saying, *"Pray this way, 'Our Father, who is in Heaven ...'"* (Matthew 6:9, my paraphrase).

As you go through the entire Lord's Prayer, you will see it is about trusting God, your Father. Jesus told us that the Father loves us, and He knows everything we need before we ask. He wants us to trust in Him every day.

Jealousy and envy flow out of a misunderstanding about ourselves as children of our heavenly Father. They come from *an orphan spirit*. Orphans believe they are on their own and must take care of themselves. Imagine you look across the street, and you see one of your neighbors driving a new car. You think to yourself, *I sure wish I had the money to drive that kind of car*. Pretty soon, you're envying your neighbor about the car. Let me ask this question: Is your Father rich? You might say, "Well, Jimmy, my father's not rich. My father has a menial job, and he's certainly not rich. He couldn't buy me a car like that." But see, I'm not talking about your earthly father. I'm talking about your heavenly Father. Is He rich? Of course, He's rich. Does He love you? Of course, He loves you. I'm not telling you He will give you that car, but I am telling you He knows all of your needs, and He wants to take care of you.

The devil wants you to go through life jealous and envious, but even more, He wants you to forget your good Father who cares for you.

———————

But you don't have to go through your life as an orphan. You have a Father who loves you.

———————

Jesus taught us to pray every day, *"Give us this day, our daily bread"* (Matthew 6:11). God is the most powerful person in the universe. He loves you, and He has a good will for your life. You don't have to envy what you don't have—someone else's relationships or belongings—because your Father has something special for *you.*

Jealousy and envy are particularly damaging if you have emotional wounds from your past. You may have lost an important relationship or gone through another type of devastating situation, such as a bankruptcy. The devil started trying to get you to focus on what everybody else had, whether it was a relationship or financial wealth. Now, because of the damage from your past, you've become hypervigilant about how you compare with everyone else. With jealousy and envy, you find yourself unable to rest, and you can't be friends with someone who has something you don't have. You've allowed the hurts of your past to become a curse.

However, you have a loving heavenly Father and the Holy Spirit inside of you who can empower you emotionally to live beyond jealousy and envy. Because of your relationship with God, now you can see someone who has something that you want and say to your Father,

If you want me to have something like that, then I think that's great. But if you don't, then I'm content being Your child. I'm content being who You want me to be and where You want me to be. I thank You that You don't love other people more because they have more money than me. You love me just the same. And I thank You that my destiny is in Your hands. I believe You will provide for me and bless me. I want to find my security in You, and not in how I compare with other people.

The apostle John says, *"perfect love casts out fear"* (1 John 4:18). I want you to know that God's perfect love also casts out jealousy and envy because they are based on the fear that you don't have enough. I remember being full of jealousy and envy earlier in my life, but I don't feel any of that today. The difference is the security I have in my Father.

You're not an orphan. You have a Father, and your Daddy can do anything in your life that needs to be done. Your life is not defined by you versus other people. Your life and your healing are defined by you relating to God. The Holy Spirit is going to completely heal all the damage of your past and close the doors the devil uses to put jealousy and envy inside you.

HEALING FROM GOD'S WORD

Who is wise and understanding among you? Let him show by good conduct that his works are done in the meekness of wisdom. But if you have bitter envy and self-seeking in your hearts, do not boast and lie against the truth. This wisdom does not descend from above, but is earthly, sensual, demonic. For where envy and self-seeking exist, confusion and every evil thing are there. But the wisdom that is from above is first pure, then peaceable, gentle, willing to yield, full of mercy and good fruits, without partiality and without hypocrisy. Now the fruit of righteousness is sown in peace by those who make peace. (James 3:13–18)

The night is far spent, the day is at hand. Therefore let us cast off the works of darkness, and let us put on the armor of light. Let us walk properly, as in the day, not in revelry and drunkenness, not in lewdness and lust, not in strife and envy. But put on the Lord Jesus Christ, and make no provision for the flesh, to fulfill its lusts. (Romans 13:12-14)

And I, brethren, could not speak to you as to spiritual people but as to carnal, as to babes in Christ. I fed you with milk and not with solid food; for until now you were not able to receive it, and even now you are still not able; for you are still carnal. For where there are envy, strife, and divisions among you, are you not carnal and behaving like mere men? (1 Corinthians 3:1-3)

And I will pray the Father, and He will give you another Helper, that He may abide with you forever—the Spirit of truth, whom the world cannot receive, because it neither sees Him nor knows Him; but you know Him, for He dwells with you and will be in you. I will not leave you orphans; I will come to you. (John 14:16-18)

HEALING TRUTHS

- We have to make a distinction between jealousy and envy. Jealousy is about relationships, while envy is about things, such as success, possessions, popularity, or advantage. Envy is almost always wrong, but jealousy can be beneficial in the right circumstances. In a righteous sense, jealousy is a protective emotion that guards the integrity of a relationship.

- Negative jealousy typically involves control rather than defending the integrity of the relationship. Jealousy becomes more severe when you have hurts from the past.

- An insecure and emotionally damaged person is much more likely to be driven by jealousy with a controlling spirit. The only relationships they feel comfortable with are those they completely control. The curse of control is that it ruins the intimacy and goodwill of the relationship. Control never works because God did not design us to dominate each other.

- Jealousy and envy are evil twins that cause us to monitor what everyone else has and everyone else's relationships with vigilance. They are fallen emotions that produce discontentment, resentment, broken relationships, and inner turmoil. When jealousy and envy motivate us to any degree, we will not be in healthy relationships with others.

- Envy is an open door for the devil to accuse us to others. Even though the only thing the other person has done wrong is to have what we want, envy doesn't make a distinction. It is a bratty emotion that believes we are the only person who truly deserves something, and that no one should have something we don't have. In a worst-case scenario, envy can even lead to theft and physical assault. That is a description of emotional immaturity, but it is the reality of our flesh.

- Jealousy and envy flow from an orphan spirit. Orphans feel alone and, therefore, they must take care of themselves at all costs. They have no sense that someone is looking out for them. Because of that distorted belief, they become hypervigilant in caring for themselves. They feel driven and cannot rest. An orphan must have too much to have enough.

- When we trust God, we don't have to focus our care upon ourselves; He cares for us. We can trust Him and believe that if He wants us to have a possession or a relationship, then He will make it happen. If He doesn't want us to have something, then we really don't want it. We must trust His plan. He loves us and wants what is best for us.

Jealousy and envy die in the presence of our Father God because we can finally rest in His love and care.

Exercises for Reflection and Discussion

1. What are your primary struggles with jealousy?

_____

_____

_____

_____

_____

_____

2. What are your primary struggles with envy?

_____

_____

_____

_____

_____

_____

3. How do you personally relate to the concept of an orphan spirit? Do you often feel as though you are on your own and you are in competition with everyone else? If so, explain.

_____

_____

_____

_____

_____

4. How does jealousy or envy change your ability to relate to others? Have you ever thought of yourself as a controlling person or as a person who is easily controlled? Explain your answers.

_____

_____

_____

_____

_____

Applying Healing Principles

Complete the following steps to apply what you have learned in the lesson:

1. **Be completely honest with God every day and in every instance when you are feeling jealous or envious.** At some point, everyone feels jealous or envious. You do not have to feel ashamed, nor is God ashamed of you. If you want to break the power of those negative emotions over you, you have to bring them to light and be honest about them. Freedom and healing begin when you are willing to make jealousy and envy open issues before God. The Lord will give you all the grace you need if you will only ask Him.

2. **Trust God with the specific issues that surround jealousy and envy in your life.** Your trust breaks the issue of control and keeps it from sabotaging your relationships. For example, if you want a relationship with someone, or you worry that you may be losing a relationship, take it to God in prayer and ask Him for His wisdom and help. This approach will keep you from being manipulative, mean-spirited, or trying to establish or keep that relationship on your own. If someone has something you want, then go to God in prayer and tell Him that you want it and then trust in Him. In the meantime, be content in your current situation. Contentment means you are happy as you are, and you trust God to give you more if He wants you to have it.

3. **Don't compare yourself with others.** The practice of comparison is the most tormenting of all because it stokes the fires of jealousy and envy. As individuals, God designed a different plan for each of our lives. If you see God blessing someone, then you should be able to rejoice with that person rather than compare yourself. God has a unique plan for you, and it is perfect for you. Comparison will keep your eyes on others in the wrong way, which promotes jealousy, envy, and many other negative emotions. Faith in God produces peace and joy and will keep you focused on Him.

Healing Confession

Confess the following aloud:

I confess, in agreement with God's Word, that I am not an orphan, nor do I have to take care of myself on my own. A gracious and loving God cares for me. He is very present and powerful in my life. I don't need to be jealous or envious of others because He loves me and cares for me. I only want what He wants in my life. I trust His plan for me and believe His desire is for me to prosper and succeed in every way.

Healing Prayer

Silently or aloud, pray this prayer:

Holy Spirit, I ask you to heal any place in me that past experi-

ences have damaged or hurt. If the devil has implanted negative messages in me through loss of relationship, rejection, or disadvantage, I pray you will expose them. Help me destroy anything that keeps me jealous or envious of others and replace those emotions with the truth of God's Word. I reject ungodly jealousy and envy in my life and thoughts. I ask You to give me the grace today to change my desires and the ability to act righteously.

Father, I come to You as my perfect, loving Dad. I know You care for me and have a plan for my life. Because of You and Your love, I am not an orphan, nor am I on my own. I trust You for every relationship, position, possession, and desire in my life. I truly don't want anything You don't want for me. I release all control to You and will no longer try to control everyone and everything around me. I surrender my life to You and trust You to guide me, guard me, and provide for me for the rest of my life. In Jesus' name, amen.

FINAL THOUGHTS ON SECTION EIGHT

The Perfect Father

When I was a young believer, one of the issues I really struggled with was my concept of God. I really didn't understand that He is my loving heavenly Father, my Daddy. Because of my misconceptions, I battled jealousy and envy. I didn't grow up in poverty, but I certainly grew up next door to it—my family wasn't wealthy. I remember envying people who had money. I don't mean that I hated them, but I did envy them. I couldn't rest in who I was in the Lord.

One day, while reading my Bible, I remember coming across a passage that discussed God's love. In Matthew chapter 6, Jesus taught about God as a Father (see vv. 25–34). As I was praying after my reading, I realized how hard it was for me to relate to God in that way. Here is what the Lord spoke to my heart: "I want you to treat Me like I'm a perfect Father, until you can prove me wrong." I wondered, *How do I treat God as a perfect father?* As I thought about it, it would mean I would have to trust Him, believe that He loves me, and really believe He is a perfect Father. He wants to take care of me as my perfect Father.

From that day forward, I began to pray differently. I started relating to God differently. I took my needs, fears, desires, and temptations all to Him. I began to act like I believed that He really is a perfect Father. Do you know what I discovered? *He really is a perfect Father!* I was able to go into His presence and have a personal relationship with Him. Jealousy and envy started to melt away. I mean, why would I be jealous and envious when I have the perfect relationship with a loving and caring Father?

Do you know He can do anything that you need? If He

wants you to have a certain friend, then He'll bring that person to you. If He doesn't, then you don't need that friend. If He wants you to have a particular possession, then He'll provide for you to have it. If He doesn't, then you shouldn't want it. The truth is that God is going to bless you because He's your perfect Father. You no longer have to go through life comparing yourself with other people. You're incredible in God's eyes. He made you special. When you have the perfect Father, that's all you need.

SECTION NINE

———

REPLACING MOURNING WITH PRAISE

The prophet Isaiah wrote about the ministry of the coming Messiah, saying He would *"console those who mourn in Zion. To give them beauty for ashes, the oil of joy for mourning, and the garment of praise for the spirit of heaviness"* (Isaiah 61:3). Do you know about the power of praise? I specifically want to tell you how it relates to depression and deep discouragement.

At times, all of us have felt discouraged, but grief doesn't go away. Isaiah says the Messiah will comfort those who mourn in Zion, which means long-term grief. The prophet promises the oil of joy for mourning, which means a deep sense of loss. You especially understand what Isaiah means if there's a sense of pain in your life that just won't go away. It may seem as if you can't grieve through it, as if a spirit of heaviness has settled upon you, and you wonder how you will ever move beyond it. Isaiah says the Messiah has a garment of praise for you.

Day 17

Dealing with Grief and Depression

Depression, deep discouragement, and constant grief can come into our lives whenever we experience moments of deep negativity. These moments open a door to the devil and allow him to whisper to us.

Tragedies like the untimely or tragic death of a loved one can cause grief and depression. I talked to a woman a few years ago who lost every close member of her family over a one-year period, and she was devastated. She wasn't simply grieving—a *deep* grief had settled over her. She said, "I'm just wondering if I should really care about anyone else in my life because it seems like everyone I care about dies." Early in this journey, I discussed whispers of hurt; this is one of them.

In painful times like these, the devil will try to embed hopeless messages of pain in your mind, telling you God doesn't love you. The devil will say you will never be able to keep anything, and you will lose everything good that ever comes into your life. At that point, you will live in constant dread, overwhelmed by a spirit of grief, just waiting for the other shoe to drop. But the prophet says the Messiah will give us "the oil of joy for mourning." That oil is the Holy Spirit. Part of His fruit is joy, and it does not depend on circumstances. Happiness depends on happenings and on things going right, but the Spirit's joy stands outside our circumstances.

You can have real joy amid difficulties.

You can experience genuine joy amid loss because your joy comes directly from the Holy Spirit.

He gives you a deep, abiding sense of wellbeing that is not tied to your circumstances. God's Word teaches us that even if we've lost something or gone through great tragedy, the answer for our grief is the sweet oil of joy for mourning that comes straight from the Holy Spirit.

Depression and heaviness can also come into our lives through either false religion or the occult. The word *occult* means "secret" or "darkness." If you have engaged in the past with witchcraft, satanism, tarot cards, Ouija boards, seances, or any sin like that, then you have opened doors for the devil to come in and oppress you. Over many years as a pastor, I have dealt with a number of people who struggled with deep depression as a direct result of occult activity in their lives. Occult activity comes from an entity outside of you. Even though it's not a part of you, it can have lasting effects on you in the form of a *spirit* of heaviness. Once you understand that, Jesus can exchange that spirit oppressing you for a garment of praise.

You may enjoy watching movies with very dark themes for entertainment, but there's a consequence to that action. When you invite demonic themes into your life, the devil will use them to oppress you. Don't be puzzled if you have nightmares after watching those kinds of movies or reading those types of books. I have adopted a basic rule when it comes to that issue: I will not pay to be scared because I can get that at no charge, just by living. Darkness and the occult invite the devil to oppress us. They can open the door for discouragement and depression in your life. Stay away from them.

Some medications may cause depression through chemical imbalances or bad interactions with other medications. If you suspect a medication is a cause, I urge you to consult your physician, and see if there are other options at your disposal. I also want to say that I have known many people whose depression was chemical, genetic, or biogenic in nature. I want to make that point clearly because the last thing I want to imply is that a depressed person isn't spiritual enough. There are people who genuinely battle depression with a sincere faith and a warrior's spirit, but they are dealing with serious physical issues also. These people deserve love, respect, and support and not judgment.

Negative words can also cause depression and deep grief in our hearts. Someone may say something like, "You'll never succeed. You'll never amount to anything. You're no good." When someone speaks those kinds of words to you, they are a curse, and they can oppress you and leave you with a spirit of heaviness. But Jesus can replace that spirit with a garment of praise as well.

The reason the prophet Isaiah calls praise a garment is because you must *put it on*. It is like dressing yourself in the morning. If I wake up and feel depressed, then I must renounce that emotion and put my eyes on God. I then open my mouth and begin to praise Him. If I'm depressed because of a tragedy in my past that I can't seem to grieve through, then I ask the Holy Spirit to come, give me joy, and heal that in my life. I must decide to "get dressed" with praise.

Sometimes, however, I become depressed because I have simply focused my eyes on my circumstances, dwelled on my past, dreaded my future, or even relived my failures. But the prophet says if I put on a garment of praise, the Messiah will take the spirit of heaviness off me. I want to remind you that heaviness, discouragement, and depression often come from the devil, and when that is the case, you can come against that demonic spirit in the name of Jesus and overcome it.

Praise is one of the most powerful things you can do. Proverbs tells us that the power of life and death is within our mouths (see Proverbs 18:21). The devil wants to take control of your tongue. He wants you to walk around the rest of your life murmuring about all your troubles and every other negative thing in the world. When you communicate that way, it just invites more darkness, and it's oppressive.

When you put on praise, however, you will wake up in the morning, and one of the first things you will do is get alone with God. Then you will begin to praise Him. Put your eyes on God. Make Him big, and your problems will become smaller. This discipline will remind you of the right things in your life, about God and how powerful He is. Next, you'll begin to feel joyful, and the heaviness will lift. You don't have to live your life depressed or with a spirit of grief. You have the power of the Holy Spirit and the power of praise in your life, and it will deliver you from a spirit of heaviness.

HEALING FROM GOD'S WORD

Bless the Lord, O my soul;
And all that is within me, bless His holy name!
Bless the Lord, O my soul,
And forget not all His benefits:
Who forgives all your iniquities,
Who heals all your diseases,
Who redeems your life from destruction,
Who crowns you with lovingkindness and tender mercies,
Who satisfies your mouth with good things,
So that your youth is renewed like the eagle's.
(Psalm 103:1–5)

When I remember these things,
I pour out my soul within me.
For I used to go with the multitude;

I went with them to the house of God,
With the voice of joy and praise,
With a multitude that kept a pilgrim feast.
Why are you cast down, O my soul?
And why are you disquieted within me?
Hope in God, for I shall yet praise Him
For the help of His countenance.
O my God, my soul is cast down within me;
Therefore I will remember You from the land of the Jordan,
And from the heights of Hermon,
From the Hill Mizar.
Deep calls unto deep at the noise of Your waterfalls;
All Your waves and billows have gone over me.
The Lord will command His lovingkindness in the daytime,
And in the night His song shall be with me. (Psalm 42:4–8)

Oh, clap your hands, all you peoples!
Shout to God with the voice of triumph!
For the Lord Most High is awesome;
He is a great King over all the earth.
He will subdue the peoples under us,
And the nations under our feet.
He will choose our inheritance for us,
The excellence of Jacob whom He loves.
God has gone up with a shout,
The Lord with the sound of a trumpet.

Sing praises to God, sing praises!
Sing praises to our King, sing praises!
For God is the King of all the earth;
Sing praises with understanding.
God reigns over the nations;
God sits on His holy throne.
The princes of the people have gathered together,
The people of the God of Abraham.
For the shields of the earth belong to God;
He is greatly exalted. (Psalm 47:1–9)

HEALING TRUTHS

- A spirit of heaviness is emotional and mental oppression that comes from the devil. The Father sent Jesus to deliver us from this oppression. With a spirit of heaviness, we may experience deep discouragement, depression, hopelessness, and even thoughts of suicide.

- A spirit of heaviness can enter our hearts through tragedy and difficulty. The devil is a hurt whisperer. In those times when you have trouble and neglect to turn to God, the devil is ready to interpret your pain for you. He always tries to embed negative and oppressive messages into our spirits. We must tear down the devil's lies and replace them with the truth.

- A spirit of heaviness can gain entry through occult practices that promote spiritual darkness. When you allow certain things into your life, such as astrology, palm reading, Ouija boards, tarot cards, seances, and witchcraft, you will face spiritual oppression. Renounce any involvement with the occult and stay away from it.

- The effects of certain medications or the interactions of multiple medications can cause a chemical imbalance that creates depression.

- Spiritual oppression can enter through negative words. Do not allow the words of others to be more important than what God says. Be careful about what you listen to and who you allow to speak into your life. Focus on good news and positive words that align with God's Word.

- The answer Jesus gives for the spirit of heaviness—whatever its source—is a garment of praise. You must put it on.

- Praise takes your eyes off of yourself and your circumstances and puts them on Jesus and what is right. It fills the atmosphere with faith and light. Praise reminds you of how great God is and how wonderful His promises are. The devil cannot function in an atmosphere of praise. A negative attitude gives an invitation to the devil to work. An attitude of praise closes the door on him.

Exercises for Reflection and Discussion

1. What are the negative experiences in your past that the devil has used to embed negative messages in you and, through them, oppress you?

_____

_____

_____

_____

_____

_____

2. List any involvement you have had with the occult or things of darkness? How has the devil oppressed you through them?

_____

_____

_____

_____

_____

3. What are the negative messages that have people have spoken to you and through which the devil oppresses you?

_____

_____

_____

_____

_____

_____

4. Do you have a positive attitude, and do you praise the Lord regularly? Or do you have a negative attitude and neglect to offer the Lord praise? Explain your answers.

_____

_____

_____

_____

_____

_____

Applying Healing Principles

Complete the following steps to apply what you have learned in the lesson:

1. **Write down any negative thoughts you struggle with and take them captive.** Renounce and replace them with God's Word. Find a verse or passage from Scripture that counters the lie and confess God's Word over your life.

2. **If you have had anything to do with the occult or spiritual darkness, then confess it to God and renounce it.** Be specific and the Lord will forgive you, and that will close the door you've opened to the devil. Take authority over any demonic spirits that are oppressing you and command them to leave you in Jesus' name.

3. **Establish a discipline of praising the Lord for at least several minutes every day. This habit is particularly important when you are struggling with your thoughts or emotions.** Praise changes everything. It uncovers the devil's tricks and neutralizes him.

4. **If you are dealing with chronic depression or feelings of hopelessness, then you must act above your emotions until they change.** Don't give in to your feelings—they are just feelings. Confess and read God's Word, then praise the Lord and obey God by faith. That will break the spirit of heaviness off your life.

Healing Confession

Confess the following aloud:

In agreement with God's Word, I confess that the Lord is worthy to be praised. The most important thing I do with my words is praise, honor, and exalt the Lord every day and thank Him for what He has done in my life. Through my praise, I defeat the enemy when he comes to oppress me or tries to get my mind and emotions focused inward and negative. I will overcome darkness with light as I praise the Lord daily.

Healing Prayer

Silently or aloud, pray this prayer:

Lord Jesus, You have empowered me through praise to overcome a spirit of heaviness. I now put on the garment of praise and put my eyes on You. I take authority over all darkness in my life as I open my mouth and release the light of Your name and Your goodness. I have allowed the devil to get me focused on myself and on negative things that have brought me down. I confess that to You, Lord, and ask You to forgive me. I have not always had my eyes on You or given You the praise You deserve. Now, Lord, I commit to You daily. I know that as I do, You will release Your life and power within me. Give me the strength to live my life to glorify You and to accomplish Your will for me. In Jesus' name, amen.

FINAL THOUGHTS ON SECTION NINE

Releasing the Oil of Joy

Sometimes when you deal with heaviness, grief, discouragement, or deep depression, it's not you. There is an outside entity. You may have experienced an awful tragedy, put your mind on dark and ungodly images, or done something else to invite a spirit of heaviness to come upon you. If you have been involved in occult practices, I'm not saying that you're of the devil or you even believe in those practices, but they will influence you, and you need to guard your environment. If you've had any attachment with the occult, then you need to renounce it because it leaves a door open to the devil. Maybe someone said something negative to you, or you've just been dwelling on your past, or you watched the news and heard something that led to discouragement and depression. All these things, and more, can invite a spirit of heaviness.

The Holy Spirit is the answer to your deep grief and depression. He gives the oil of joy for sadness or mourning. Let Him come into your life and bring the fruit of the spirit, which includes joy. When you focus on God and invite the Holy Spirit to come into your emotions, He will make you joyful.

The devil wants you to take your eyes off God, but praise puts your eyes on God. When you praise God, He will change your negative outlook into a positive one. Praise is not merely another religious activity. It is warfare against the devil, while negativity is his language. He wants you to focus on everything wrong in and around you and uses others to give you a gloomy outlook. However, praise helps you focus on God and breaks off that spirit of heaviness. It is a garment, but you won't wake up with it on. You must *choose* to put it on to protect yourself against the devil's spirit of heaviness.

SECTION TEN

PEACE THROUGH PRAYER

The result of inner healing is the ever-present peace of God, a deeply powerful inner sense of wellbeing. Jesus said, *"Peace I leave with you, My peace I give to you; not as the world gives do I give to you. Let not your heart be troubled, neither let it be afraid"* (John 14:27).

Day 18

Pray Until Peace Comes

The apostle Paul wrote, *"Be anxious for nothing, but in every-thing by prayer and supplication, with thanksgiving, let your request be made known to God; and the peace of God which passes all understanding, will guard your hearts and minds through Christ Jesus"* (Philippians 4:6–7).

Paul gave two directives when he wrote to the Philippian believers. First, he told them not to worry about anything—*be anxious for nothing*. Some people don't believe that is possible. They might say, "I'm kind of a nervous person. I mean, it's just the way that I am. I've got a lot of anxiety." But Paul was serious about what he wrote, and God won't tell you to do something in His Word that is impossible to do. The Bible wouldn't tell you to not be anxious for anything if you couldn't do it. Therefore, Paul gives a second directive that will help you to accomplish the first: Put prayer into every situation in your life. That is how you let God know what concerns you. With prayer and supplication, you communicate to Him what you want and need. You do all of that with a spirit of thanksgiving—gratitude for what God has done and *will do* in your life. Remember how good He has been, and thank Him in advance for how good He's going to be in the future. You can have great confidence in your loving Father because He is so good and loves you so much.

I don't have to pray a nervous prayer to try to get God as upset as I am. (Though, I admit that I have done that in the past.) What I do is pray to my loving Daddy, and thank Him for listening and acting. I know my Father cares about me, and He's going to answer my prayer, so I make a conscious choice not to be anxious about anything. While He works, He gives me a peace beyond all comprehension, meaning that sometimes, I can't even understand why I have so much peace. The Lord guards my heart, emotions, and mind as I surrender my anxiety to Him. The Greek word translated "guard" means a military sentry who protects me from an outside enemy.

Some of the things we face are part of who we are, but many of our negative emotions come from the outside. For example, the spirits of fear and heaviness don't come from you because that's not the way God created you. They come from the devil—he is trying to get your eyes off of God so you will live a defeated and ineffective life.

Worry and anxiety also come from the devil. That doesn't mean you can't worry on your own, but the enemy wants to put a spirit of worry and anxiety upon you to wear you out.

Let your worry list become your prayer list. Prayer is one of the most practical things you can do for your own well-being. Some people say, "I don't pray very much. I'm just not a real religious person." Prayer is not about being a religious person; it is a very practical act.

The peace of God is available to you when you choose to pray and trust God.

When you choose to set your worry and anxiety aside and let God put a military guard around your mind and emotions, the devil can't slip in and put anxiety on you. That is how you live in the peace of God.

Worry can ruin your marriage, your relationships, and your health. Many of the doctor's office visits people have are because of stress and worry. We are wearing our bodies out. But God didn't design us to worry all the time. He created us to live in peace. The truth is that if you don't pray, then you *are* going to worry. If you take your concerns to God and believe He will do those things you can't do, then worry can't be a constant companion for you.

You may wonder, "Well, Jimmy, how do I know if I've prayed enough?" I encourage you to pray until you get peace. Pray for your children until you get peace. Pray about your finances until you get peace. Pray about demanding situations until you get peace. Anytime something worries you, pray until you get peace. The peace you receive is God telling you, "I heard your prayers, and I'm going to protect you and take care of you." I write down everything I am worried about, and that becomes my prayer list. Then, I pray until I get the peace of God.

Jesus said, *"if two of you agree on earth concerning anything that they ask, it will be done for them by My Father in heaven. For where two or three are gathered together in My name, I am there in the midst of them."* (Matthew 18:19-20). If you will join in prayer with one or two other believers, it is even more powerful than praying on your own. Karen and I realized a long time ago that when we don't pray, that's when the devil comes in and accesses our hurts, worries, and fears, and we end up fighting. Together, we decide to overcome any anxiety or worry the devil tries to put on us by agreeing together in prayer to trust God.

HEALING FROM GOD'S WORD

For unto us a Child is born,
Unto us a Son is given;
And the government will be upon His shoulder.
And His name will be called
Wonderful, Counselor, Mighty God,
Everlasting Father, Prince of Peace.
Of the increase of His government and peace
There will be no end,
Upon the throne of David and over His kingdom,
To order it and establish it with judgment and justice
From that time forward, even forever. The zeal of the

Lord of hosts will perform this. (Isaiah 9:6–7)

Peace I leave with you, My peace I give to you; not as the world gives do I give to you. Let not your heart be troubled, neither let it be afraid. (John 14:27)

And let the peace of God rule in your hearts, to which also you were called in one body; and be thankful. (Colossians 3:15)

Therefore humble yourselves under the mighty hand of God, that He may exalt you in due time, casting all your care upon Him, for He cares for you. (1 Peter 5:6–7)

Be anxious for nothing, but in everything by prayer and supplication, with thanksgiving, let your requests be made known to God; and the peace of God, which surpasses all understanding, will guard your hearts and minds through Christ Jesus. (Philippians 4:6–7)

HEALING TRUTHS

- It may seem as though anxiety is a condition and not a choice, but we can choose to be anxious, or we can choose to be at peace.

- We must make a daily decision not to worry and to pray instead. Our old worry list should become our new prayer list.

- The benefit of prayer is the peace of God. This isn't peace the way many people think about it; it is an enormously powerful peace. According to Paul, when we trust God in prayer, His peace guards our hearts and minds like a sentry protects against an enemy's military invasion.

- This peace God promises is so profound that it surpasses all understanding. That means sometimes, you won't be able to figure out why you feel so much peace. In the natural, you may think you should be nervous, but you're at a perfect peace that bypasses your intellect. It is not because you finally got everything figured out, but because you're trusting God to figure it out.

- Prayer doesn't work unless there is a transference of trust. It doesn't matter how much you pray about your problems if you don't transfer the burden to the Lord. Paul tells us we must pray with a spirit of thanksgiving. Not only do we thank God for what He has done, but we are also thankful in advance that He is going to answer our prayers in the present and future.

- One of the reasons we tend to worry rather than pray is

that we don't understand how incredibly caring God is. He is very present in our lives and loves being our Father. The Lord is generous, doting, and powerful. He is the ultimate Father who wants to walk through the circumstances of our lives with us.

Exercises for Reflection and Discussion

1. List the things that cause you to be most anxious right now. This is your new prayer list.

_____

_____

_____

_____

_____

_____

2. What would you say is your main challenge in truly trusting God with the issues of your life?

_____

_____

_____

_____

_____

_____

3. List the negative effects of worry and anxiety in your life.

_____

_____

_____

_____

_____

4. How would you describe your belief in God's love? How would you describe your faith in God's Word as it relates to prayer?

_____

_____

_____

_____

_____

Applying Healing Principles

Complete the following steps to apply what you have learned in the lesson:

1. **Pray over your list of worries and anxieties every day *until you get peace.*** Go to God with every issue and trust Him. Thank Him for being a perfect Father. Additionally, thank God in advance because you know He will take care of you.

2. **Begin to see anxiety as an enemy and an open door for the devil's attacks.** Be militant as you refuse to live an anxious life. Take your anxieties and worries before the Lord in prayer every day. God designed us to live in His abiding peace. When something disturbs your peace, it is a warning sign, and you must take it seriously before the Lord in prayer.

Healing Confession

Confess the following aloud:

I confess, in agreement with God's Word, that He designed me to live in peace. I will not allow anxiety to rob me of that peace or of my relationship with Him. Rather, I will trust God with the problems and issues of my life. I will take my cares before Him because He cares for me as my loving Father. I will live in the peace that comes from trusting God as He guards over my mind and heart.

Healing Prayer

Silently or aloud, pray this prayer:

Father, I come to You with all the worries and anxieties of my life. It is foolish for me to be worried and anxious when I have such a caring Father like You. You are powerful enough to easily solve any issue in my life, and I thank You in advance for hearing and answering my prayers. I repent for the sins of worry and unbelief. I now trust You to give me wisdom, provision, and guidance. I trust You to take care of the problems that are too big for me and are beyond any human ability to solve. Nothing is impossible with You. I transfer the burden of my needs to You and pray You will give me Your peace. In Jesus' name, amen.

FINAL THOUGHTS ON SECTION TEN

Your Loving Daddy Cares

Part of the ongoing process of becoming a healthy person, both emotionally and spiritually, is focusing our attention on God and trusting Him. God loves you and loves being in relationship with you. He intimately knows about all your problems and wants to be involved in your life because He cares about you. The apostle Peter says to *"cast all your cares upon the Lord because he cares about you"* (1 Peter 5:7, my paraphrase). When you pray, you're not talking to a disinterested party somewhere up in the sky. You are talking to your loving Daddy.

Anxiety is not a condition; it's a choice. You can choose not to be anxious. When your anxiety goes away, and the peace of God replaces it, then it will change your physical body, every relationship in your life, and everything else. God's peace is going to heal you, and you're going to stay healed for the rest of your life. Anxiety is not who you are. It comes from the devil, and he wants to keep you from being the person God made you to be. Your loving Father says you don't need to be anxious any longer. He will give you a powerful, incredible peace and put a military guard around your mind and emotions.

SECTION ELEVEN

THE POWER OF PERSONAL ACCOUNTABILITY

The apostle Paul told Corinthian believers, *"Do not be deceived: 'Evil company corrupts good habits.'"* (I Corinthians 15:33). The truth is, your friends are your future. There are some things God will only do through the relationships that you have. You will never be healthy long-term if you develop unhealthy relationships. When you put yourself in the presence of people who tempt you to sin, engage in negative behavior, are ungodly, or are unrighteous, then it's really going to complicate your life. You need good people in your life, and you need personal accountability.

Day 19

You Need God's People

When Karen and I first got married, I was a very private person. We started going to church and got involved in a Bible study group where we got to know some people. We'd been having some marital problems, and one morning, I said some pretty mean things to her. That afternoon, she informed me that we were going out that night with our Bible study teachers and that she had told them all about our problems. I was sure I was going to die right there.

Over dinner, our Bible study teachers lovingly told us they had some of the very same problems when they first got married. Then they offered us some incredibly good advice that night that helped us tremendously. Karen's willingness to reach out to someone for accountability was a great help.

A few years later, we changed churches, but I still was a very private person and didn't want to get involved the way we had in our previous church. I wanted my relationships to stay on the surface. But, once again, Karen signed us up for a discipleship group. I still had some serious issues I didn't want anyone to know about. I thought if I just attended the regular worship services and didn't get to know anyone, my secrets would be safe. No one would find out how messed up I really was.

But we got involved in that discipleship group of thirteen members. It's hard to hide in that small of a group. Right off the bat, the leader of the group said, "Well, can anyone in here play guitar and lead worship?" Karen spoke up and said, "Jimmy can." I was really struggling to have good feelings about my wife at that point. I didn't want to lead worship in that group. In fact, I didn't want to be in that group in the first place! But let me say this; it transformed our lives. I soon found out that everyone else in the group was as messed up as I was.

We grew to love the people in that group. We talked about everything and prayed for each other. Three years later, the church called me to be their pastor. I don't think I would be where I am today without that group. I needed those close relationships. In fact, the closest relationships I've ever had have been in the church. My best friends came from the church. And those relationships kept me accountable, helped me pray through situations, gave me godly wisdom, and helped me heal.

Many of the greatest things God will do in your life will be in atmosphere of healthy relationships.

I realize no one's perfect, but believers share a common

faith. And most of them are trying to do the right thing as they serve the Lord and support each other in the process. Don't let the devil get you alone. Don't separate yourself away from church and other believers, and especially, don't connect to unhealthy relationships. Your friends are your future. *"Don't be deceived. Bad company corrupts good morals."* All of us have issues and need each other, and we need an environment of accountability.

One of the best things that ever happened to me was because my wife insisted that we get involved at church. Her decision led to me becoming the person I am today. God used that environment to help me, heal me, grow me, and put me in an environment of accountability. There, God was able to do what He wanted to do in my life.

You can't do what God has called you to do alone—the devil is a wolf, and a wolf always looks for the lone sheep. You need a godly, Bible-believing church to help you build relationships and keep each other accountable. You won't find perfect people, but you will find people who are trying to live for God like you, and He is going to do some of the most powerful things in your life through those relationships.

HEALING FROM GOD'S WORD

Let us hold fast the confession of our hope without wavering, for He who promised is faithful. And let us consider one another in order to stir up love and good works, not forsaking the assembling of ourselves together, as is the manner of some, but exhorting one another, and so much the more as you see the Day approaching. (Hebrews 10:23–25)

Do not be deceived: "Evil company corrupts good habits." (1 Corinthians 15:33)

Is anyone among you suffering? Let him pray. Is anyone cheerful? Let him sing psalms. Is anyone among you sick? Let him call for the elders of the church, and let them pray over him, anointing him with oil in the name of the Lord. And the prayer of faith will save the sick, and the Lord will raise him up. And if he has committed sins, he will be forgiven. Confess your trespasses to one another, and pray for one another, that you may be healed. The effective, fervent prayer of a righteous man avails much. (James 5:13–16)

For by one Spirit we were all baptized into one body— whether Jews or Greeks, whether slaves or free—and have all been made to drink into one Spirit. For in fact the body is not one member but many. If the foot should say, "Because I am not a hand, I am not of the body," is it therefore not of the body? And if the ear should say, "Because I am not an eye, I am not of the body," is it therefore not of the body? If the whole body were an eye, where would be the hearing? If the whole were hearing, where would be the smelling? But now God has set the members, each one of them, in the body just as He pleased. And if they were all one member, where would the body be? But now indeed there are many members, yet one body. And the eye cannot say to the hand, "I have no need of you"; nor again the head to the feet, "I have no need of you." No, much rather, those members of the body which seem to be weaker are necessary. (1 Corinthians 12:13–22)

HEALING TRUTHS

- Relationships and accountability with other believers are essential to living a victorious Christian life. The devil wants you to be prideful and isolated. The Lord wants you to be humble and accountable.

- The Lord does His greatest work in our lives when we are in close relationships with fellow believers. In terms of our emotional health and well-being, one of the best things we can do is be around people who encourage and love us.

- When we are going through challenging times, it is crucial to have someone to talk or who will pray with us. It can mean the difference between victory or failure and hope or hopelessness.

- Don't be ashamed of the things that are going on in your life. We all have the same basic struggles. You need to find someone to talk to and pray with about what you are going through. You need close Christian relationships that you are regularly nurturing. You don't have to tell everyone in your life about everything that is going on, but you do need to tell someone.

- When a wolf is looking for a sheep to devour, he looks for the loner. Wolves never attack sheep that the shepherd gathers around himself. That is exactly what happens when we get into fellowship with other believers. We gather around God and help each other through life's struggles.

Exercises for Reflection and Discussion

1. What are the best relationships you have with other believers? What relationships do you need to nurture and develop?

_____

_____

_____

_____

_____

_____

2. What are the worst relationships you have that bring you down and have a bad influence on you?

_____

_____

_____

_____

_____

_____

3. What are your main fears in telling others about your struggles or in asking for help?

_____

_____

_____

_____

_____

_____

_____

4. Do you see getting help as something for the weak or the wise? Explain your answer.

_____

_____

_____

_____

_____

_____

Applying Healing Principles

Complete the following steps to apply what you have learned in the lesson:

1. **Get involved in Christian relationships.** You do not get the full benefit of being a member of a church if you don't have close relationships with other believers. Get out of your comfort zone and into your church. Regularly attend the main worship services and a small group where you can build relationships.

2. **If there is an area in your life in which you chronically struggle or feel overwhelmed, talk to a believer, and ask**

that person to pray with you. You can select a pastor, a leader, a mature believer, or a close Christian friend, but it needs to be someone who won't judge you or respond negatively to you.

3. **Decide that you will never again isolate yourself and become unaccountable when you are struggling.** If you associate with people who are negative, hurtful, or ungodly, then you might consider cutting off or minimizing those relationships. You need to build good relationships and minimize negative ones to stay emotionally healthy.

Healing Confession

Confess the following aloud:

I agree with God's Word and confess that I need other believers in my life. I know God never intended for me to go through life's problems alone. Even though God does so much in my life, I recognize there are things He will only do through other believers. I will not be ashamed of the struggles I experience, and I will not be afraid to have relationships with other believers. I will be honest and accountable as I ask for prayer, help, and encouragement when I need it.

Healing Prayer

Silently or aloud, pray this prayer.

Father in Heaven, I accept my need for Christian fellowship and accountability. As I seek to grow in this area, I ask You to lead me to the right people and the right church. I come against all my fears and objections in Jesus' name. I realize the devil wants to use them to keep me isolated, but I make the choice to have a committed connection to a local church and to build relationships there. I pray You will supernaturally lead me in that process. Heal anything from my past that the devil would try to exploit to keep me from this commitment. In the process, make me into a person who can help others overcome their own struggles as well. In Jesus' name, amen.

FINAL THOUGHTS ON SECTION ELEVEN

Don't Go It Alone

When Karen insisted that we get involved in a church and a small group, I was afraid, but it saved my life. I discovered all of us need each other—no one is the exception to that rule. If you don't have quality relationships with other believers in your life, then you need to find a good local church, where you can find a Bible study, a small group, or another way to get to know other Christians well. As you grow in your relationship with them, you don't have to tell *everyone* your problems, but you do need to find someone you can talk to, with whom you can pray, who can hold you accountable if you're struggling in an area.

All of our closest friends are those we met in church, and those rich relationships changed our lives. They invested so much in us, but we've been able to invest in them as well.

That's the kind of environment that God wants you to have because those relationships will make all the difference in the world and keep you on the road to being the person that God wants you to be. If you're struggling with a particular issue, then don't struggle alone. What you can't do alone, you can do in relationship with other people. If you're going through something right now, seek out a pastor, leader, or another mature believer you can trust. You might begin by simply asking, "Hey, would you pray with me?"

SECTION TWELVE

A LIFE OF HEALING AND HEALTH

Emotional health means you can *relate to others, get through conflict properly,* and *process negative emotions the right way.* When you are not emotionally healthy, you won't have those abilities.

Day 20

Evaluating Your Emotional Health

The following test will help you determine your level of emotional health. Answer all 18 questions honestly, without laboring long over your answers. Each question contains a scale from 0 to 10, with 0 meaning you don't possess that particular ability and 10 meaning you are extremely healthy in a particular area.

Your aggregate score is not relevant for this evaluation; it doesn't matter how it all adds up. Rather, look at the score of each individual question. If you score high in an area, then it means that you are healthy in that area. If you score low, don't allow your scores to discourage you. It simply means that you have an area that needs change. Any score can change very quickly, depending on the circumstances.

If you score from 7 to 10 on a question, then it means you are healthy in that area. If you score from 4 to 6, you will want to take note of it and work on that area. If you score from 0 to 3, it means your relationships are likely suffering, and you need immediate attention in that area. You may need a counselor, pastor, or another mature believer who can walk with you as you journey toward healing in that area. If you score low in any area, don't give in to discouragement. Your scores are not etched in stone; they are just a baseline and could improve dramatically over the course of just a few weeks or months.

I want you to take this test again a month from now, or two months. Focus on those areas with the lowest scores. Work on them, pray about them, and let the Lord heal you in those areas.

Emotional Health Inventory

Circle (select) one number between 0 and 10 on each issue. 0 being the least healthy and 10 being the healthiest.

1. My ability to openly express affection, both physically and verbally, to the satisfaction of those closest to me.

   0 1 2 3 4 5 6 7 8 9 10

2. My ability to empathize with others and focus on the needs and desires of others—especially those closest to me.

   0 1 2 3 4 5 6 7 8 9 10

3. My ability to communicate honestly and openly in a gracious manner.

   0 1 2 3 4 5 6 7 8 9 10

4. My ability to express valid complaints and confront my family and others in a timely and gracious manner.

   0 1 2 3 4 5 6 7 8 9 10

5. My ability to receive complaints, correction, and input in a gracious manner without being defensive or hostile.

   0 1 2 3 4 5 6 7 8 9 10

6. My ability to take responsibility for my behavior and say that I am sorry with sincerity and grace and in a timely manner.

   0 1 2 3 4 5 6 7 8 9 10

7. My ability to serve and give to others who do not reciprocate—especially those closest to me.

   0 1 2 3 4 5 6 7 8 9 10

8. My ability to process anger, offenses, and disappointments in a timely and gracious manner.

   0 1 2 3 4 5 6 7 8 9 10

9. My ability to be vulnerable and reveal weakness without fear or shame.

   0 1 2 3 4 5 6 7 8 9 10

10. My ability to be joyful and faith-filled during difficulty, and see the good in things and people.

    0 1 2 3 4 5 6 7 8 9 10

11. My ability to rejoice and be gracious with those who have gained wealth, status, or some other advantage.

    0 1 2 3 4 5 6 7 8 9 10

12. My ability to compete and win or lose in a gracious and humble manner.

    0 1 2 3 4 5 6 7 8 9 10

13. My ability to laugh at myself and keep a sense of humor about life, even amid difficulty.

    0 1 2 3 4 5 6 7 8 9 10

14. My ability to trust God with the hurts, needs, and desires of my life and to rest in His love.

0 1 2 3 4 5 6 7 8 9 10

15. My ability to control my temper and my tongue during conflict and anger.

0 1 2 3 4 5 6 7 8 9 10

16. My ability to relate closely to others without controlling them or being controlled by them in a wrong manner.

0 1 2 3 4 5 6 7 8 9 10

17. My ability to exercise authority or advantage over others in a righteous and humble manner.

0 1 2 3 4 5 6 7 8 9 10

18. My ability to submit to authority humbly and respectfully, even when I believe those in that position are wrong.

0 1 2 3 4 5 6 7 8 9 10

Applying Healing Principles

Complete the following steps to apply what you have learned in the lesson:

1. **Make a list of your answers with the five lowest scores.**

A. _____

B. _____

C. _____

D. _____

E. _____

2. **From the list of your answers with the five lowest scores, pray about how you can address those areas, and make three action points that will help you grow for each of them.** For example, if you scored low on being physically and verbally affectionate, then one of your action points might be to express physical and verbal affection to every person in your home daily. Your action points should take you out of your comfort zone and give you something specific to do to.

A. _____

    i. _____

ii. _____

iii. _____

B. _____

    i. _____

    ii. _____

    iii. _____

C. _____

    i. _____

    ii. _____

    iii. _____

D. _____

    i. _____

    ii. _____

    iii. _____

E. _____

    i. _____

    ii. _____

    iii. _____

Come back to these action points on a regular basis to remind yourself and stay accountable. After some time, re-take the test to see if any of your scores have changed. Once again, list three action points on your five lowest scores and work on growing in those areas. Your goal is to be healthy in every area. Remember, a low score means you and those around you experience the negative effects of your behavior. Emotional health reflects your ability to relate to God and others positively in both good times and bad.

Emotionally healthy people have successful relationships and can weather the inevitable storms of life with faith and grace. Regardless of where you are now, you are going to grow to become the person God wants you to be.

Healing Prayer

Silently or aloud, pray this prayer.

Heavenly Father, help me to change. You have done so much in my life as I have been reading the lessons in this book, and I want to continue the journey to healing and freedom. I want to be a different person, the person You want me to be. I ask You to give me the power and grace to change and grow until I am completely emotionally healed and whole. Help me face my fears and work on the areas where I am the weakest. I ask for Your supernatural grace to flow through me so I can heal and grow in every area in my life. In Jesus' name, amen.

Day 21

The Ongoing Journey

My prayer is that God has done a work in your life as you have journeyed with me through this book and that your investment of time and faith will pay off in fantastic dividends. As I said at the beginning, return to these lessons as often as necessary and use what you have learned to help others find healing.

I don't want you to feel euphoria at the changes you have experienced, only to forget about it in a few days.

Decide that you are going to be a different person for the rest of your life.

I know the difference between those who stay healed and those who don't, so I want to conclude by reminding you about three important decisions you must make to remain healed for a lifetime.

THREE IMPORTANT DECISIONS

1. Stay Close to God

First, stay close to God and grow in your relationship with Him. You aren't simply being healed from something, you are being healed *to Someone*, and that is God. Bondage keeps you from being the person God made you to be, but Jesus healed you, and now you are free to love and serve Him.

Jesus went alone to quiet places to spend time with the Father, and Jesus is your example. He commands us to go to a secret place to spend time alone with God (see Matthew 6:6). This is a foundational discipline for freedom, and it protects our personal relationship with God and nurtures our ability to hear Him when He speaks.

Personally, I begin with praying the Lord's Prayer, using it to worship the Lord and acknowledge His will in my life. I submit myself to the Lord and ask Him to tell me anything I need to be doing to follow His will. I pray about all the needs I have. I pray the Lord will forgive me, just as I pray for Him to reveal and help me correct any relationship in my life that isn't right. I forgive every single day—I don't want to live one day of my life in unforgiveness. I ask the Lord to lead me every day in the paths He wants me to travel. I want Him to go with me and to protect me from all the evil that the devil would try to do. I ask Him to protect my family and pray for all the people I care about.

For over 48 years, Karen and I have spent quiet time alone

with the Lord every day. The length of time we spend may vary – but doing it every day is critical. I read my Bible, both Old and New Testaments. I also write in a journal about anything significant that is happening in my life. Do what works for you; the main thing to remember is that you need to talk to God every day. Prayer is a dialogue, not a monologue. God speaks your language, so listen to His still, small voice as He speaks to your heart. You will know His voice because it agrees with the Bible, is always loving, and is always gracious. Write down what you believe God is saying to you. Ask Him to heal your hurts. Take your fears and anxieties to Him. Trust God with everything you care about. When you start your day pursuing the Lord, you will have a lifeline of hope, healing, and love all day long.

2. Maintain Godly Friends

The second critical habit of staying healed is to have godly friends who support your faith. The apostle Paul said, *"Do not be deceived: 'Evil company corrupts good habits'"* (1 Corinthians 15:33). As I told you in Day 19, your friends are your future. If you believe you can have bad friends and live a good life, then you're deceived. Whenever you find a group of people practicing sin, they will want you to do what they're doing. If you don't, they'll likely persecute you.

When the Lord first saved me, I was 19, and I had ten close friends who I'd had since elementary school. The day the Lord saved me, the first thing He said was, "Never see your friends again." And I didn't. I look back now and realize that it was a good thing I listened to the Lord because my friends did not turn to Christ and would have ruined me. A few of them even persecuted me later because I was living for the Lord. Two of them died of alcoholism in their thirties, and others had very destructive lifestyles.

You need a support group if you're going to live in health and freedom. You need to have people around you who will support your faith and hold you accountable as you grow.

3. Be a Part of a Bible-Believing Church

You may already be a part of a Bible-believing church, but if you aren't, find one, join it, and be committed to it. Where do you think you find good friends? You primarily find them in church. As I told you earlier, when I first got saved, I didn't have any Christian friends. The only friends I had were Karen and Jesus. We started going to church, and though I didn't like Christians or church, Karen really kept encouraging me. I stuck it out and met the best people I've ever known. You're going to find your best friends as well.

I am certain that no one can successfully live for Jesus long-term without being in church. You may ask, "Do you mean I can't be a Christian without being in church?" I believe the Lord can still save you, but a Christian, by definition, is a person who follows Jesus. The world is very evil. It is too easy to fall away from the Lord without accountability. You need a place full of loving people who support and encourage you in your faith—that is what church is for.

If you have a personal relationship with Jesus, strong Christian friends, and you're a committed part of a healthy, Bible-believing church, then you're going to be healthy and free. You may have challenges, but you're going to get through them. You're going to succeed and overcome any hardship because you're living the way you should.

HEALING FROM GOD'S WORD

But you, when you pray, go into your room, and when you have shut your door, pray to your Father who is in the secret place; and your Father who sees in secret will reward you openly. (Matthew 6:6)

Do not be deceived: "Evil company corrupts good habits." (1 Corinthians 15:33)

Do not be unequally yoked together with unbelievers. For what fellowship has righteousness with lawlessness? And what communion has light with darkness? (2 Corinthians 6:14)

And let us consider one another in order to stir up love and good works, not forsaking the assembling of ourselves together, as is the manner of some, but exhort-

ing one another, and so much the more as you see the Day approaching. (Hebrews 10:24–25)

HEALING TRUTHS

- Jesus promises us complete healing, and that is a wonderful experience.

- Once we are healed, we must establish three crucial disciplines in our lives that will keep us in an atmosphere where our health and freedom can continue under protection. The three disciplines that create a fortress of healing and freedom in our lives are a personal, daily pursuit of God; close friendships with godly people who share and support our faith; and being a committed part of a local, Bible-believing church. These three things are essential for every believer who wants to live for God and create a legacy of healing and emotional health.

Exercises for Reflection and Discussion

1. What is the best time of the day for you to have a quiet time with the Lord? What would you like your quiet time to look like, and what do you need to make it happen daily?

_____

_____

_____

_____

_____

2. Do you have any relationships that you need to break off?
If so, from whom? How and when do you plan to deal with
those relationships?

_____

_____

_____

_____

_____

_____

3. Do you have healthy Christian friendships? What do you
need to do to develop strong friendships with fellow believers and strengthen your commitment to your church?

_____

_____

_____

_____

_____

_____

4. What has the Lord done in your life throughout these 21 lessons? Summarize your experience and the important things God has done in your life through this time.

_____

_____

_____

_____

_____

_____

Healing Confession

Confess the following aloud:

I confess with my mouth that I am totally and permanently healed. Jesus has healed me, and I will now protect this health for the rest of my life. I will not take it for granted and go back to old patterns of life that caused my problems. I am a new *person, and I will develop new disciplines in my life to protect my health. I am committed to having a daily, private, quiet time where I will pray, read my Bible, and seek God. I am committed to developing and maintaining strong Christian friendships and to being a dedicated part of my local church. I will make whatever changes and sacrifices are necessary to make sure these new disciplines are a permanent part of my life.*

Healing Prayer

Silently or aloud, pray this prayer:

Lord, I thank You so much for being with me through these 21 lessons. I especially thank You for what You have done in my life. I cherish Your love for me and all that You have done to change me. I now commit to living my life to serve and please You. I will not take my healing for granted or go back to my old ways. I commit my life to You. I am your disciple, and I want to live a life of discipline and obedience. Give me the power to change and break old habits. As I commit to seeking you in a daily quiet time, I pray You will reveal Yourself to me and speak to me personally. Lead me as I seek to know You and trust You in every area of my life. I pray You will help me develop strong Christian friendships and find the right church for me. I trust You to sovereignly lead me and orchestrate circumstances in my life to take me where You want me to go and meet the people with whom You want me in relationship. The rest of my life is about loving and serving You. I praise You and thank You for everything You have done for me. I will tell others about You and be a witness for You. In Jesus' name, amen!

FINAL THOUGHTS ON SECTION TWELVE

The Blessing of Healing

We're at the end of our journey, but continue to make changes as the Lord leads you. I'm so proud of you!

I hope you've been blessed by this book; it's been my privilege to write it for you. It took me years to get free because I just didn't know, and I wish someone had taught me what I have been telling you. Now, you know that you can be healed as you live your life the way God intended. Your legacy is different now because you've gone on this journey. It will change you, your family, your children, and your grandchildren.

I want to pray for you and bless you:

Father, in the name of Jesus, I bless my friends who are reading this right now, a blessing of complete healing. I pray you would bless them with life, prosperity, favor, opportunity, promotion, good relationships, and fruitfulness. I ask that You would bless them in their going out, in their coming in, in their lying down, and in their rising up. Lift Your counte-

nance upon them, Lord, and give them peace for the rest of their lives. I declare over them that their legacy is one of healing and emotional health. From this day forward, they're going to live their lives as healthy people. Form them into the people You created them to be. I bless them in Jesus' name, amen.

God bless you.

TIPS FOR SMALL GROUP USE

- *Plan well, but allow the Holy Spirit to change your plans.* As members of your group confront the pain and hurt from their past, you may need to take more time than you originally planned. Don't force the group to move on when you need to dig deeper into a particular area.

- *Create a safe environment.* Some group members may need to share some very deep things with the entire group, while others may want to keep their thoughts and feelings more private. Allow room for differences, even when group members write their answers down in their workbooks.

- *Allow time to respond.* As you go through the exercises, pause when you ask questions and don't try to answer questions for the group. This may seem awkward in the beginning, but it will allow the members of the group time to consider their words carefully.

- *Listen intently.* Don't plan what you are going to say next while members of the group are still talking about a previous issue. Let the responses of the group members shape what you will discuss next. Listen with compassion because some strong emotions will be expressed as the group members go through these lessons.

- *Guard your own opinions carefully.* There is a time to teach and time to listen. Don't answer your own questions, at least not until everyone else has had an opportunity to respond. If you give your own answers too quickly, it will stifle the conversation.

- *Model respect.* Make sure each person has an opportunity to speak and be heard, and respect those who do not wish to speak.

- *Let prayer be your guide.* Group members will express many beliefs, opinions, and feelings. Ask God to give you discernment for how to respond to anything that will be expressed in the group.

- *Follow up.* After the session is over, some group members will have additional questions and need ongoing attention or accountability. Remember, the primary goal is healing and relationships; getting through the material is secondary.

ABOUT THE AUTHOR

 Jimmy Evans is a long-time pastor, Bible teacher, and best-selling author. He is the Founder and President of XO Marriage, a ministry devoted to helping couples thrive in strong and fulfilling marriages. Along with his wife, Karen, he is the host of *MarriageToday with Jimmy & Karen*, a nationally syndicated broadcast television program as well as a weekly podcast with the same name. For 30 years, Jimmy ministered as Senior Pastor of Trinity Fellowship Church in Amarillo, Texas, where he now serves as Apostolic Elder. He speaks at dozens of live events every year to tens of thousands of people. Jimmy has written more than 17 books, including *Marriage on the Rock*, *The Four Laws of Love*, *Strengths Based Marriage*, and *Tipping Point*. Jimmy and Karen have been married for 48 years and have two married children and five grandchildren.

REAL TESTIMONIES FROM PEOPLE WHO COMPLETED THE 21 DAY INNER HEALING JOURNEY

"It is very personal and deep, like counseling, but I can do it at home."

"Each day's teaching is short and straight to the point while also being very clear and easy to follow and understand."

"The 21 Day Journey is very doable for busy people! It has the right amount of structure and freedom!"

"I realized I was living my life based on emotions. This has helped me in my marriage and my relationships with other people by doing what is right despite my emotions."

"I learned so much about how God sees me and how He loves me. I never realized the concepts I had about God were so negative until going through this journey. Now I know He loves me!"

"It has been like standing in front of a mirror and seeing all the things I didn't know were on my shoulders."

"It brought me a lot of hope when I thought God didn't care

about me and all that I have been going through these last few years."

"There are truths we know but need to be reacquainted with daily. The course was simple but profound. Life changing for my whole family."

"I wasn't aware of how much my unforgiveness triggered my anxiety, but now that I've completed the journey, I am more at peace than I have been in a long time and working daily on forgiving."

"Immediately, I could feel how cathartic it was to be reaching back into the past and confronting things that happened that contributed to the person I grew up to be as well as why I have made some of the harmful decisions. By Day 7, I was able to get through the lessons without tears. That's when I realized that God really was working with me on this."

"I enjoyed the insight and breakthrough to better emotional health. It has already started to improve the way I relate to myself and others, and I know this is just the beginning of a positive change. I have spent thousands of dollars on counseling to overcoming my past, and I feel this course accomplished even more. I already understood many of the concepts from Christian counseling and over 40 years of daily Bible reading, but this resource took my healing to the next level."

"Overall, the content was phenomenal. Scripture-based, practical, and Spirit-led. God spoke to me each day of the journey. It was challenging, yet so gracious and loving."

"This course made me feel normal and not alone."

"For so many years I struggled with the same emotional deficiencies and not knowing how to change. I would pray and see some change but eventually fall back into bad habits. This changed when I realized and then really believed my Heavenly Father truly loved and accepted me. I'm not perfect, but I enjoyed the thought-provoking questions about the inner pain I've felt. I feel that the course helped me fix my eyes on Jesus and His full healing!"

"I liked the writing and praying and breaking down the reasons for feeling deep rejection."

"I have learned a lot about myself. I have found where my deepest hurts originated, and I am dealing with them daily. I feel happier and freer since doing this. I will definitely do it again."

"I loved the simplicity and how the written material fostered looking inwardly with the Word to see what the areas of weakness are and what steps to take to allow the Word to do what God intended."

"I really enjoyed evaluating every area of my life and learning more about God and how our relationship should work. My relationship with God is what will improve my relationship with others."

"I really enjoyed the freedom I felt after each lesson. I experienced REAL healing. It was as if I could literally feel God operating on my heart. I also enjoyed being able to work through this at my own pace. My journey was longer than 21 days (way longer), and I appreciated knowing that it was okay to take my time. Some days I had to go back and redo a day, and that was fine. The journey was tailored to fit my needs, and I'm glad that I wasn't put in a box. My special needs were honored, and for that I am most grateful."

"A practical application for emotions and how they affect our relationships. The incorporation of Scripture was beneficial as instruction (that is, teaching rather than preaching)."

"Completely opened my eyes and shifted me."

"It drew me closer to God in my everyday walk."

"There was so much Scripture to back up the lessons. I really like the Healing Truths sections because it helped me to be able to put into words what I need to say out loud."

"I went through the course with my daughter-in-law at a time when she and my son were at an impasse. Things have turned around for them in so many ways. My husband has also done the course with our son."

"It has opened my eyes to so many things about myself and my view of God. It truly has healed so many broken things in my heart. It will be a study that I do over and over until I am completely healed. I thank God for me finding Jimmy on YouTube. My marriage and family were destroyed by Satan's lies. My husband and I are doing the Marriage on the Rock program and both of these studies have literally saved my marriage, healed my soul, and are restoring my family. I now have faith God can and will heal my family and repair the damage I have allowed Satan to do in my life. God always wins!"

"Jimmy explains and interprets the Bible so we can understand like never before."'

"It was a great refresher course for living as a Christian. It kept my eyes focused on my wounds and what needed to be healed in me. I like the survey at the end as well, which allowed for good discussions and opening myself up to hear my family members share how they see me."

"There was never a day when I didn't glean something from the lessons."

"This experience has caused me to pause and think about things from the past that I had yet to forgive because I had buried them in my memory for so long."

"This experience has showed me some of the issues that I am still dealing with. Pride, not forgiving my dad, and shame. It has also shown me the power of God's Word and the tricks Satan uses to keep me from being who God wants me to be."

"I liked that there were a lot of things I had never thought about before."

"It helped me realize how anxiety is a choice that I can choose daily to overcome with opposition from the Word of God."

"Loved the Power of Praise chapter. For some reason this teaching really hit me over the head with the revelation that I let the devil make me think I didn't deserve things, like to dream, to lose weight, and be in my appropriate weight range...etc."

"I have been going through heavy depression. My life has been in turmoil during this time. God led me to this program which has been a tremendous source of healing for me."

"Love the insights that are not so commonly understood."

Exclusively on

XO Now

The 21 Day Inner Healing Journey is also a unique online experience that offers hours of video content from Jimmy Evans, daily plans and personal application exercises that will guide you through deep emotional healing and into total freedom.

Visit XONow.com to sign up today!